Thirteen to Nineteen

Julian Sleigh

Thirteen to Nineteen

Discovering the light

Floris Books

First published in 1982 by Floris Books
Third edition published in 1998 by Floris Books
Fifth printing 2002

British Library CIP data available

ISBN 0-86315-283-X

Printed in Europe

Contents

Foreword

No book can deal adequately with the theme of adolescence, and I have done no more than share thoughts and ideas distilled from my own experience of parenting teenagers. I have, however, hoped to help all who would read this book to value and enjoy the wonder of the teen years, in spite of the difficult transition they span.

I had thought of calling this book 'Sailing Through the Teen Years' but realized that this would give the impression of an easy passage. Nevertheless, I have kept the sailing idiom for the chapter headings.

My warm appreciation goes to Lin Zimbler, who worked through the contents with me, offering many essential suggestions; and to Nina Rowley, who in typing the manuscript asked a great number of questions that led to improving the text; and also to my wife Renate and our five very individual children, who have carried me through this phase of parenting with unbelievable endurance!

Julian Sleigh

1. Setting sail

No transition is easy, and the seven years that lead from being a child to entering adulthood are uniquely intensive. We shall try and search together to review the events that point to the mysterious and deep movements of soul within a person during the teen years. There are difficulties, but they do not need to be blocks that eclipse the light that shines in at this time: like shadows they can awaken us to the light behind them. The teenage years can be enjoyed by teenagers and by parents. These years see much growing and unfolding; as each step is welcomed, it can be understood. All too often it is the difficulties that stand in the foreground and gain prominence and not the incredible revelations that occur in these years.

Thoughts and feelings that I share with you do not come from a professional base: I am neither a teacher nor a psychologist. My main source of inspiration is my family of five children and the love that weaves between us. The first three daughters and the son are already through their teen years; only the youngest daughter has still (at the time of writing) two years to go. They were born within the space of ten years; yet each has found a different way through the maze of adolescence; the variations were dramatic.

My wife and I tried to provide them with a secure and appropriate childhood; our work within a residential community in a rural setting afforded a favourable background. There was sunshine and nature, and our children could enjoy an out-of-doors life with plenty of swimming and riding. There was security, religion, festivals, country life, yet within reach a beautiful city (Cape Town). We made time for each other in spite of our demanding work. The children grew up surrounded by friends and had the companionship of other children of their own age. They had devoted teachers, and they had opportunities to develop their musical and artistic talents and their social and practical skills. Yet choppy seas, at times very rough ones, awaited them as each in turn set out beyond the sheltered bay of childhood.

Our eldest daughter suffered from learning difficulties and could not cope with her school work; she had to go away from home at the age of twelve to a remedial school. This raised a few new problems at the outset: the kind person who offered to care for her turned out to be an alcoholic. Although our daughter gained scholastically through the specialized tuition, she was still deeply unhappy with her school experiences and left early to work on a farm with relatives in Northern Ireland. So she spent nearly four of her teen years away from home, always somewhat burdened by a feeling of non-achievement. Yet through all this there has grown in her an insight into human nature, and she has since blossomed into a perceptive and sensitive person. She has overcome most of her learning problems and has developed her natural artistic abilities. These she has put to good use: she has qualified in jewellery-making and interior design. The bumpy periods during most of her adolescence were the cause of a great deal of anxiety, and we as parents felt powerless to alleviate the inner pain of her struggles.

Our second daughter had an excellent track record in school and seemed well on the way towards an academic career; but she became pregnant at sixteen-and-a-half. The following year had to be divided between motherhood and Matric. All plans for further study had to be abandoned. In the years that would normally have belonged to a widening of experience of the world and of herself, she was catapulted into adulthood and had quickly to establish herself. Marriage came at twenty-one and more children have made her life one solely of motherhood. But all these tests have brought out the strong mettle of her personality.

The other members of the family have had exposure to drugs and alcohol. This seems inevitable in the later teens (if not already in the early teens as well), but they have been able to turn from these allurements and stabilize themselves, developing in the process strong social impulses. The third daughter studied sociology and now works in conflict resolution in the townships, a highly relevant task in the Cape Town area at the present time. Our son has made his tour of Europe and has qualified as a chef; he has experienced the stresses of a high-pressure restaurant kitchen. He also worked for a while as a barman in a London nightclub, seeing there the often forced jocularity of the escapists and the sadness of people without purpose or companionship. He had witnessed all this before the end of his teens. The next step has been to go to university and study social science. Our youngest daughter has completed schooling successfully and her main aims are independence and the acquiring of practical skills. But becoming free from school has raised the need for commitment to training and earning.

It was fortunate that the channel of communication between our children and ourselves as parents never closed. Moreover, they helped each other. They each had their own circle of friends with whom they could evaluate their experiences. And they could see that, in spite of the fact that we did not always enjoy what they had to go through, we trusted an inherent guidance which would lead them rightly. There has emerged in each of them the awareness that a young person is responsible for his or her own life and must be prepared to meet challenges with the resources that each has acquired. We felt reassured when we saw this: our efforts to bring up our children in a right way had after all not been wasted. As children they had depended on what was given to them. Now they are on their way to being adults on whom others can depend.

Our family had so much in its favour, but has not been spared the tribulations: how much greater must be the teenage trials that confront a family that is not so favoured! How can we ensure that the claim made at the beginning of this chapter can be proved true: 'The teenage years can be enjoyed'?

2. Millstream or maelstrom

Adolescence is a dramatic time for any young person: it is so for the parents as well. One way of understanding the upheaval of the teenage period is to look at what happens to parents during this period. The changes which take place affect them very much: their whole being is challenged, sometimes to the very core.

Parents will be able to cope with the challenges if they become aware of their own attitudes and observe their reactions. For example, their worries. Parents tend to worry when the teenager scene approaches: they know their child will be exposed to many dangers. But every step in life has its dangers: why the particular worries around this one?

There are the obvious worries, but the more subtle reasons for being insecure have to do with their own peace of mind. A teenager begins to come close and hold up a mirror. Parents find themselves looking back over their own lives: the mirror doesn't reflect them as they *are* but as they *were* themselves as teenagers. Maybe for the first time they can now look back and ask: 'How was it with *my* adolescence? Have I fully come to terms with the issues that stirred in me then? Were there areas of fear and guilt which I suppressed, either because I felt I should or because others made me do so? And now that I face the adolescent stage in my son or daughter, is it these unresolved emotions that are rising up in me?' The parent may project such emotions on to his teenager, and not accept them as belonging nearer home. But he will get further if he is able to take the mirror and see himself.

Overreacting is a pointer to unresolved conflicts in one-self. The threat that the adolescent poses becomes less if the parent acknowledges his or her own locked-up stresses and strives to resolve them. The peace that will eventually result from this will be thanks to the fact that there is a teenager in the family!

Then there can well be the fear of losing control over the son or daughter. It is so important to address this fear if it lurks in one's soul, and be very honest about it. The parent has been sovereign to the child but he cannot simply rule the adolescent. All parents go through the agonizing process of realizing that they no longer have full control. Does this mean that they must abdicate? Many parents do. But if the *sovereignty* is changed into *supportive guidance,* a new relationship comes about. The symbol for sovereignty is the king, and what is needed to replace it has more to do with caring, supporting and accompanying. This gives rise to the image of the shepherd.

So the picture comes to mind of kings and shepherds. The qualities of being a king have to do with authority and the power to assert that authority whenever necessary. To gain and maintain this authority the king has to have knowledge and wisdom and also strong self-discipline. He is looked upon as an example. He has to be wise enough to listen to inner guidance as well as information and opinion, and be able to make decisions uninfluenced by desire for power or personal gain. A king has to be a philosopher and warrior, a judge and a counsellor, a ruler and a servant bearing the destiny of his people. He also has to be enlightened enough to welcome the growing to maturity of his crown prince and others of his progeny, consciously preparing them for the task that they will carry on into the future. The kingly quality engenders order *and* freedom at the same time. His head is crowned to indicate the nobility and wealth of his thinking power. He wears rich garments and lives in a palace.

The shepherd knows his terrain and his sheep: for both he has the right interest and feels the right love. He is peaceful in himself and peacefulness comes about around him; this helps his sheep to thrive. He keeps an eye on the weather and knows how to work with the changing seasons of the year: he also guards the sheep against the wolf that lurks unseen. He cares, and feels, and so engages the qualities of his heart in what he does for his sheep. His garments are homespun, hardy and meant for being out in the open; and his dwelling will be a cottage near the pastures.

Parents, can you identify yourselves with some of these qualities? And which ones in particular, those of the king or of the shepherd? Though ideally both parents should have both sets of qualities in the right mix, one could say that *children* need to meet the kingly quality in the father and the shepherd in the mother. Then with adolescence the parents should merge these qualities and both be 'kingly shepherds'. The growing person seeks for sovereignty, self-control and self-knowledge in those who are to be his examples. He does not want to feel ruled: he looks for persons who, by being sovereign over themselves, are able to give him the protection he needs without depriving him of his freedom. The young child needs to be com*mande*d; he gains security from the authority of his parents. The adolescent should rather be com*mende*d; he thrives on the guidance *and praise* that his parents give him.* This is the meaning of 'supportive guidance'.

All this has further significance for the adjustment parents have to face at this transition. The idea of king or queen

---

* I have tended to speak of the teenager as 'him', except where the context indicates the need to distinguish between 'him' and 'her'.

has in it the principle of a right to determine the life of the subject. While the child is young, the parents have this right, tempered by responsibility to the divine for the way it is exercised. Once their child becomes adolescent, the parents' responsibility remains but the idea of a right to determine his life is no longer acceptable. Resistance to it necessarily begins to grow. Parents may feel anguish at first at this rejection and at their loss of control; they may indeed feel very inadequate in the face of what is taking place.

They can go through a dreadful time when their teenager becomes rude, rebellious, revoltingly clever, messy, moody, and no longer that beautiful child of whom they were so proud. Oh, the non-stop pop music, the tousled hairstyle, the impossible way of dressing, the jeans that are either faded and torn or garish and slinky. The sudden appearance of all kinds of bangles, pendants, earrings, nose studs, (goodness — what next!) *tattoos!* This after the caring and conscientious upbringing, the training in good manners, the cultivated behaviour, the unbounded affection.

What a jolt to the pride of the parents! Till then the child reflected the quality of the upbringing. What hurts all the more is that the arguments begin. Father finds that his son has become so clever he can dispute things better than father can. And surly with it. What is worse, the arguments turn on the very things that the parents prize most: their religious ideas, their political convictions, what they like in the way of art and music: it is as if whatever the parents particularly value will be subject to scathing indifference or even declared hostility. If the beliefs, standpoints and values of the parents are not well-founded, their teenager will gently (or not so gently) show up the weaknesses: it may not come to an argument, but it will be very obvious that the teenager has suspended the hitherto-unquestioning allegiance to what the parents hold dear. The less sure they are of the foundation of their beliefs, the more effective the attacks. If the parents have not really come to grips with their own standpoints in the areas at issue, they are in for a rough time.

Three subjects that are not usually welcomed at the dinner table will be the areas of greatest challenge: religion, politics and sex. Certainly they *do* need to be spoken about openly and freely; any shying-off from wanting to discuss these issues could show the parents up as having not quite worked through their own confusions. Attitudes that have persisted since their childhood without becoming truly their own, or that have been taken over from what they have read or from the church they attend, will be exposed to a barrage of piercing questions, or be ignored. Parental pride and outlook can be shaken through all this.

If, on the other hand, the adolescent sees that his parents are not stuck, that they still continually review what they value and deepen their grasp of these three subjects, then there will be less cause for criticism. The young person will instead feel encouraged to turn to them with genuine questions. And if he meets with an honest admission of shaky areas and unresolved quandaries, together with an openness to listen, he will respond with interest and even gratitude for being allowed to share in the searching of his parents.

All this can be very stimulating, very renewing, for parents. Clichés, dogmas, habitual modes of thought and socially-conditioned attitudes, unexamined beliefs, standpoints based on subtle unadmitted snobbery, these will all wither under the penetrating gaze of a teenager. When a child is born the parents can know that they have twelve years of grace during which the child will not question the integrity of their beliefs and habits. But after this any inadequacies will be exposed. The teenager will, however, be able to accept weaknesses if the parents acknowledge them.

It is not perfection that wins the day, but sincerity and congruence.

Another strong emotion that a parent may have to face is shame. The young person does not only question the parent's way of life: in some respects he or she may well adopt it. Again the parent looks into the mirror that his teenager holds up for him, and sees the reflection of his own habits and weaknesses. He may see himself smoking and drinking; he may hear his own bad language; he may recognize his own deviations from what he would wish to be like, his own double standards, his own thwarted ambition. All this is uncomfortable. The parent can no longer say: 'Do as I say.' He won't succeed until he can change this to: 'Do as I do.'

Any cover-up, any pretending to be what one is not, or using someone else's thoughts without making them one's own, or clinging to habits because they are socially useful, will run the risk of being shown up. The adolescent is insecure because he is overwhelmed by the whole new world that has opened to him: so he looks for security in people and ideas that he can trust. And this means testing out. He will look for this security first in his parents. If he does not find it there, his disappointment will be agonizing and the parents will have to admit to themselves: 'He does not find us to be the people he thought we were.' He will in any case also look elsewhere. He may succeed in finding what he is looking for, but in the process his connection with his parents will have suffered a setback.

Even if there is no disappointment with his parents, the teenager will at times turn to other people for inspiration and guidance, and if they become the focus of his love and admiration, the parents may feel bereft, discredited and bypassed in an area where there should have been till then a satisfying fulfilment. It is uncomfortable for parents if the teenager has turned away from them because of their inadequacy. But turning to other people does not always imply rejection of parents. In a healthy situation it becomes a natural development: horizons are widening, new spheres of interest are opening up, and new guides are needed. Wise parents can rejoice at this development.

It is particularly poignant when parents are made to feel 'past it' because of their age. Their son or daughter may admire a younger womanhood than the mother's, or a more virile manhood than the father's.

When the children form strong relationships outside the family and pursue them with intensity, the mother may feel she is just a provider. The teenager becomes skilful, and his skills could outstrip those of the parents. Parents will now have to be prepared for uncomfortable moments when they will suddenly realize that their sons and daughters can already do some things better than they can.

Moreover the pattern for holidays has to change: even the pattern for outings, for walks in the woods, and helping in the garden. The teenagers detach themselves and do their own thing. While the teenagers are still at home they may be very demanding, needing all kinds of things from Dad and Mum, like the loan of the car, more pocket money, or permission to go on a jaunt with questionable company. To say nothing of wanting a motorbike! The adolescent yearns to be free of restrictions, although he knows he still depends on his parents.

All these situations call upon parents to consider the attitudes they will adopt in the face of these changes in their children.

So the roles of parents change when their children become teenagers. Caring and nurturing do not come to an end but shift. It is the emerging personality rather than the physical being of the person that asks for attention: parents confront a unique, different person manifesting new traits, gifts and weaknesses. The new 'being' is tender and sensitive as it emerges, and may adopt an armour of brashness, even of aggressiveness, to begin with. Parents with insight will see through the armour and meet the nascent being with respect, interest and sensitive regard; in a word, with love.

3. Keeping steady

How, then, can parents prepare themselves for the growing freedom of their children in adolescence?

There are no simple answers. The parents of teenagers are in for a turbulent time. But those who examine their own attitudes and emotional reactions make the first step towards coping. When they have understood and come to terms with their fears, resentments, worries and indeed their dislikes, they can go further. There are more questions to be asked. What about love? The parents must ask: 'Do I love my teenage son or daughter *unconditionally?*' If as parents you find that your power to love depends on good behaviour, on gaining right responses, on the absence of actions which are threatening to the accepted order, then you are not loving unconditionally. Can you go on loving your teenage child when he or she has transgressed the rules that you live by or the values that you hold dear when it happens that the teenager brings dishonour to the family and causes friends and acquaintances to be negative about your way of bringing up your children and your loss of control over them? Will such experiences lower the tone of your love for them? In theory it is easy to say 'Not at all'; but in practice, when things go wrong, will your love be able to withstand anger and hurt? Will there be a moment of stress when you will say 'I don't love you' to your child? Or else, 'If you conform to what I require, then I will love you'? If this is so, then you have not really grasped the meaning of love. 'Love is not love which alters when it alteration finds.'*

Loving is not the same as liking or enjoying. Love is that positive force that forms and supports the inner core of the person loved and helps it to radiate through his being. You cannot expect a feedback to love: it has to be given freely. And when your teenage son or daughter has transgressed or is in trouble, then your love really has meaning: for then it is needed more than ever, and its withdrawal can break the spirit of the one who is struggling. The finest moments in life come through crises rightly handled, and indeed the greatest progress comes about in this way: progress in relationship and in understanding life. The unloving parent who expresses disapproval of wrongdoing may get his point across, but his connection to the child will suffer in the process. The loving parent may find his viewpoint understood without words, and his connection to his child will be strengthened as a result of what they share together.

And with love goes trust. It is easy to trust the trustworthy: there is no great merit in doing this. But to trust the person who could let you down makes trust real and turns it into a force that can bring a good influence to his intentions and deeds. Such trust reaches through to a depth that was not accessible to the person himself, and opens the way for him to get there on his own.

And so becoming a parent of a teenager means examining the force of love and the power of trust in yourself. This self-examining helps towards self-knowledge. The message com-

---

*   Love is not love
     Which alters when it alteration finds,
     Or bends with the remover to remove:
     O no; it is an ever-fixed mark
     That looks on tempests, and is never shaken ...
          Shakespeare, *Sonnet CXVI*

ing through sounds like this: If you can understand yourself, you will understand the teenager in your family. Search for the unfinished business within you: your resentments, your sense of failure, your wounds. Be honest with yourself.

See if you are able to talk with your son or daughter without barriers. If your responses are free of yes-buts and you can truly listen, then you will know that you are on the right path. The teenager does not expect his parents to be like God, but to be true and at peace with themselves. He will love you for being uncomplicated in the way you listen and speak; honest in facing your own weaknesses and his; disciplined in the way you handle your life, your tasks and your career; straight in the way that you speak, so that those with whom you speak know where they are with you. He will inwardly rejoice when he sees you maintaining your cheerfulness in the face of difficulties, because this shows your trust in a higher strength that is certain to win through. He will look for your ability to change, and will be thrilled if he finds that you are not fixed. He may not want to hear about your ideals, but they will speak to him when you live by them. He will be inspired by recognizing that you have a vision which gives direction and focus to your life and are prepared to suffer in order to keep faith with it. He will be happy if he finds that there is no cynicism in your attitude to your fellow men. In so far as you can live up to his expectations, you can answer his needs and ease his passage through adolescence; this will in turn make life easier for you.

Parents, you do well to avoid being over-anxious, monitoring and watching the activities of your teenage children. Honour their need for privacy and secrets; do not pry and wish to be party to everything that is going on. It is better to be warmly interested in what they *do* want to share with you. They don't always wish to reveal all that is still moving in a tender way in their thoughts and feelings: the first time of falling in love, the cherished photograph. Don't be upset by garish posters of a pop singer hero who plainly lacks all the qualities that you hold dear. Don't be shocked. Try to understand every phenomenal surprise. Bear with the music as best you can.

Above all, allow your son or daughter to run some risks and make mistakes, though don't hesitate to tell him or her where you see the dangers, what your own experiences have taught you, and why a different course of action would be better. But let this be objective and not rising out of some unclear emotion within you. Take a long view: thirteen to nineteen is a passage with many changes; and, given space to grow, your son or daughter will pass through the phases required by the teenage scene and peer group pressure. If your channel of communication is open, he or she will use it when in need. Don't try to retain total control; rather be close and available.

Do you remember how you managed with *your* old-fashioned parents? What did you most want from them in those turbulent years when you started to find yourself? Accept that your relationship with your children can seldom be *very* good during these years, but it can be *good enough*. When things go wrong, take time to see why they did go wrong, and learn from the experience. Always be prepared to change your attitudes. Examine yourself to see how you use your leisure, what props you require and on what you are dependent.

Your children will ask even more than this from you. You need to trust in the power that will guide them through these times; you can only do this by strengthening your own contact with the divine in yourself. And this means strengthening your inner life.

Work together as parents, sharing deeply your response

to all that happens. Your marriage will take on a new rich-
ness through strengthening your teamwork, and your other
children will thrive in the purposeful atmosphere of your
home.

When you discuss anything with your teenage children,
do so with due regard for the individuality that is emerging
within them. Your regard will help their selfhood to emerge,
and what grows in them may prove greater than you ever
expected.

An overall guiding word would be 'praise'. Praise every
achievement, every evidence of growth in your son or
daughter. But praise, too, their struggles and even their failures, for they point the way to achievement in the future.
And don't only praise *them:* accept their praise for you
when there is occasion for it.

4. Into the head wind

The New Testament contains many deep mysteries and wonderful insights into the human soul, often told in simple terms. The second chapter of St Luke depicts Jesus as a boy and gives a striking description of the impact of adolescence.

Jesus was in his thirteenth year when he went to Jerusalem with his family for the spring festival. When his mother and father set out on the way home, they were not worried that Jesus was not with them; but during the first day of the journey they began to search for him in the party, and did not find him. And so they went back to Jerusalem. For three days they looked for him, and then found him in the Temple, conversing with the teachers. These learned people were amazed at his knowledge.

When Mary and Joseph found him there, they were clearly upset, and a scene takes place that tells much about the quickening of adolescence. Mary the Mother exclaims: 'Child, why did you do this to us? We have spent three days looking for you and have been very worried.' And Jesus replies: 'Why did you look for me?' and he adds: 'Did you not know that I had to be busy with the affairs of my Father?' Here we see a new stand: sudden total independence from the parents, even with what seems to be a lack of concern; this comes with an unexpected opening of the mind to deep knowledge. There is no feeling that what he has done needs to be forgiven: he is even surprised that they should find it unusual behaviour. Jesus speaks with complete conviction about what he is doing, because this is what he is meant to do, and he refers to another authority, whom he calls 'my father', whose realm he has to serve.

This was far from easy for his parents to accept. It invalidated their protective, concerned control, and it seemed they were not even to be referred to; there was another Father. 'Did you not know?' says the young person.

The entry into adolescence is seldom so marked and precipitate. When a young person soars from childhood to youth, it usually takes more than three days. But it doesn't take all that much longer.

In the story of Jesus, there follows another phase of adolescence. He immediately left this special place and his new-found companions and went 'down' with his mother and father to their home in Nazareth. A comet-like rise to spiritual heights was followed by a return to his earthly home.

From this point on, Jesus had two homes: his spiritual house, in which he could dwell in sublime thoughts of his own, though this had at first to be in secret; and his earthly house, embedded in a family, with duties towards his parents and teachers. He would work with his father and learn his trade, and share his tender thoughts with his mother. The father found a companion, and the mother was no longer having to care physically but could carry in her heart all that was growing and blossoming in the soul of her son.

There remains alive in Jesus the striving for wisdom and the unfolding of strength, but with it a quality of reverence towards God and his fellow men, in particular towards his parents.

Here then, is a picture of the onset of adolescence, the birth of a new Person, who from now on will live into the person whom the parents conceived, bore and nurtured. A spiritual being begins to take hold of the earthly one. There is an explosion of consciousness: a sudden expansion of knowledge, a quickening of interest in the visible and also the invisible realms of life. It is like a conception. The heavenly, eternal, infinitely valuable spirit-being now begins to make its abode in the house that it has built with the help of the parents, teachers and all others who cooperated. The child in this thirteenth year goes *into the temple* and is quickened by his own divine spark. These are the moments when he enters the world of God. They can be brought on by becoming lost in wonder at some sight of great beauty, like a sunset or a waterfall. There may be many such moments.

What happens is astonishing. That which reveals itself in an instant needs then to be gathered up again, as the child touched by his own higher being returns home to the place of his parents. There a new phase begins: quietly this divine element within him takes hold of him and changes him, prepares him for his destiny and begins to reveal to him what his destiny is. This shows itself in the way the adolescent begins to form his ideals and his values independently from his parents: he begins to develop a potential that cannot be explained by heredity. Gradually he forms the aims which will guide him towards the study he will want to make, the training he will decide to go through, and the career he is probably going to select by the time his teen years are complete.

What now comes from within the young person transcends what he has received through heredity and environment, and this needs to be respected by parents and teachers and helped by the quality of education. The way to facilitate this meeting of person-to-person and avoid any hindering of the growing 'I' is discussed in the final chapters of this book especially Chapter 11, 'Coming Alongside'.

The picture of a cross emerges: there is the balance

between the horizontal beam, all that has to do with heredity and environment, and the vertical beam that represents one's higher being, descending direct from the spiritual world. Using this image we can say that the onset of adolescence brings the sudden awareness of the vertical element as it begins to affect and interact with the horizontal one: the struggle in the years of adolescence is to achieve a balance between these two, and in adult life after that there comes the further need to maintain this balance in a dynamic partnership. The horizontal beam represents that which is vulnerable, prone to ill health and has a limited span of years. The other is eternal, always intact, radiant and true.

The temporal element becomes enlivened and free through the radiance of the timeless spiritual element, and it is this that enables the human being to fulfil the purpose of his life. Where the two beams cross is the place of consciousness. At this place the young person enters a holy space for an instant and can experience the eternal now, and can then begin to develop in himself a feeling for what is true, good and beautiful.

During childhood the spiritual element shines above the child like a star. St Matthew describes the star that came to rest over the house where the young Child was. With this Child the star was visible to the wise kings and came to rest above an earthly building: and with all children the star is there even if we have no eyes to see it, resting above the house of their earthly body. With the onset of puberty the star begins to penetrate the house, revealing its wisdom and enabling the child to become aware that he has 'another Father'. But then must come obedience and the growth in stature and wisdom: in other words the bringing together of these two streams so that the one does not overwhelm or eclipse the other.

The stirring up of so much darkness at the onset of adolescence is a sign that something truly spiritual is happening. The dark forces do their utmost to stop this fusion taking place in a harmonious way. The modern adolescent is tempted to pry into the spirit world by taking drugs, which only succeed in giving him hallucinations. The miracle of puberty unleashes darkness and dangers, but is itself a release of *spiritual* energy.

With the attainment of puberty, consciousness of objective experiences is suddenly joined by awareness of the subjective. The adolescent has to meet the subjective element that wells up and let it mix and merge with the objective. The facts of one's environment, the weather, the shape of buildings, the friends who live nearby, are suddenly seen differently, more keenly and deeply, because of what they mean to the inner life of feeling. The weather will be an outer symbol of an inner mood; forms and structures will arouse feelings of aesthetic beauty or be seen as ugly, all this reflecting the inner sensitivity that is awakening. Friendships will take on depths of intimacy, sharing and reflecting. So the young teenager searches for his or her best friend, usually one of the same sex. This friendship becomes the channel through which the inner feelings can be expressed. To have no best friend causes serious deprivation in a person whose subjective life is beginning to awaken.

Adolescence is a time of expansion but also of contraction, of new strength but also of timidity. There is the stirring of a love for beauty and a fascination with ugliness, a search for values and a drastic discarding of what exists in the established order. There is a dramatic expansion of intelligence, but it is in danger of being stultified by drugs and alcohol. Ideals are born within the person, but also cynicism. He has the longing to become a true person but cannot yet trust his own worth. The adolescent seeks for independence but knows that he needs support. He rejects his parents' authority but seeks their approval. His accustomed order and rhythm succumbs to chaos and untidiness.

Feeling the spiritual stirring within him, he looks for purity in relationship, and yet he begins to experiment with sex. He wants to put the world right, but often tends rather to destroy all that exists. He wants to be one with the adults around him but knows that he is not yet mature. He seeks for a faith but rejects religion. He can be hurtful in his criticism of others, and yet is devastated when approval is withheld from him. He is continually challenging his parents to leave him free, but would be lost without their support. He longs to assert himself but feels small in a world that has suddenly become big around him. He adopts a separate culture, often alien to his parents, but wants to be understood.

5. Studying the charts

All personal development takes place in three distinct but interweaving spheres. There is the physical manifestation, the soul or personality growth, and spiritual unfolding. Adolescence is a period of intense development in all three spheres. The changes in the body, soul and spirit of a young person during the teen years bear witness to the birth of the Self. This new selfhood calls forth the interaction of these three elements. The body, as it grows and changes, provides the vehicle or vessel for the soul, which in turn provides the forces to be used by the spirit. The spirit is the eternal divine entity that permeates the soul and body. This fine and sensitive process is fostered or inhibited by the state of well-being of the body and of the soul. The way the body is fed, the rhythms of its routines and the culture of its environment will all influence the fine tuning of the body as an instrument. This in turn affects the way the soul-forces of thinking, feeling and willing can work in it. And in response come the even finer and more subtle prompting, inspirations and impulses of the individual spirit.

The scenario laid out here can only be a general survey. Each person's voyage through adolescence will be different. For some the running may go smoothly, while others may have to battle against heavy winds.

The course is charted somewhat arbitrarily, the stages

being set out year by year. Some young people will progress more rapidly than others, but in general all follow the same course.

Thirteen

In the first years of adolescence the young person begins to turn inward and enter at certain times into a secluded world of his own. At other times he balances this turning inward by applying himself with intense interest to his surroundings, showing a voracious appetite for knowledge and an amazing energy for becoming engrossed in assignments that appeal to him. And so there grows in him an interplay between the outer and inner, as if all that is outer derives its meaning from the way it feeds and expands the inner. The person leaving childhood behind becomes reflective. Actions become more conscious. The longing for independence and solitude emerges. With this can grow embarrassment at anything sentimental, a shying away from expressions of affection, for instance from his parents, as if to say: 'Don't touch me; I have not yet become firm in my new state.' The process of learning to live with himself has begun and is still tender.

Underlying this turning inward is the awareness of the changes in the physical body. The first experiences of erection and menstruation quietly indicate the emerging forces that awaken powers of great mystery and consequence. Embarrassment, worry, the need to reflect on all that begins to transact in the deeply personal areas of being, make the young teenager seek the protection of solitude; but at the same time he longs for the chance to express and talk over what is moving in his soul.

The parents may find him suddenly moody and unso-
cial, withdrawn and hard to reach, and because this is a
new turn in his behaviour, they may not know at first how
to respond: they may make remarks that drive the young
person further into himself. The parents need to show
that they are full of understanding for what is happening
and respect the emergence of a new sensitivity in their
son or daughter. If they allow themselves to express their
feeling of regard, they w ill help him greatly, for this will
give him the confidence to share what is working within
him.

Fourteen

As adolescence progresses a happier period follows. The
turning inward has had its effect, and the young person
becomes more ready to face the world and to feel part of
it. A greater robustness replaces the earlier tenderness.
Physical growth is well on the way, in terms of height and
sexual development. The sexual aspect becomes less
mysterious as the identity as feminine or masculine
becomes more clearly defined, and the function connected with this identity more acceptable.

Generally at this stage the young person is glad to be
who he or she is. There is enjoyment, laughter, sociabil-
ity and a more relaxed emotional state. Being less tense
and sensitive, the young person enjoys discussions, even
good-natured arguments, because he revels in his growing
powers of thinking. He is now more able to analyse,
weigh up, see various sides of a proposition, and reach a
conclusion that is intellectually satisfying. This is
enriched by the budding of ideas and greater fluency in
speaking. The child is now disappearing. In a boy the

voice is deepening and the facial features are changing: it is an in-between stage. The girl develops womanly features which give a fair idea of what her appearance will be in later years.

It is an optimistic phase. The young person at this age asks for more individualized guidance, because he is becoming aware of his individuality. When confronted (even critically) he is now less daunted, because any unfair criticism will be seen as such and challenged with a newly developed reasoning power. Any giftedness is by now revealing itself: one can feel the person coming into his or her own. He or she begins to make judgments about what is good or beautiful, and the sprouting of a moral sense and an aesthetic feeling gives new substance to the soul life.

Parents do well at this stage to give their son or daughter increased responsibility, but they need to be on the alert to ensure that they do not ask too much.

Against the generally optimistic background of this stage of adolescence, they need to observe whether their son or daughter is accepted in the peer group. With a boy the groups tend to be quite large, whilst the girl needs one, two or three close girlfriends, with whom she can share her thoughts, feelings and observations in their never-ending flow: the times spent together in school breaks are followed up by long sessions on the phone in the evenings, when in hushed tones all the events of the day are examined and appraised. Parents therefore need to worry if their fourteen-year-old son is not taken up in any peer group or their daughter has no friend. A family move to a new area can put a severe strain on the daughter, when from one day to the next she is suddenly deprived of the hour-by-hour contact with her small intimate structure of friends.

The initial introversion of thirteen should be followed within a year by an opening out to enjoy all that is going on at fourteen. If it is not, parents need to be particularly supportive of the self-image of their son or daughter. At this, just as at any other stage in life, one's self-esteem is largely based on what persons, whom one values, think of one. And so the esteem that parents have for their son or daughter in early adolescence will help him or her to build up the feeling of self-worth. Not much needs to be *said:* what parents *feel* will communicate deeply. But occasionally one has also to say it: 'We value all that is *you.*'

Fourteen is also the threshold between the second and third seven-year period in the biography of the person. (We go into this in more detail in Chapter Six.)

Fifteen

We now enter the middle ground of adolescence: fifteen. The burst of exuberance gives way to the emergence of the most precious power of soul life, *feeling.* As it quickens it can 'convey a melancholy into all our day'* — not sadness or despondency, but a sense of detachment and a reluctance to put into words all that begins, still tentatively, to move within. It is not so much the discovery of the inner subjective world, more a wanting to become aware of a new discovery in one's own self, the heart. It is as if you see a majestic landscape stretched out before you: there it lies; how magnificent and breathtaking! Then you regain your breath and begin to savour the finer atmosphere that is engendered by the view; you breathe with it: the movement

---

* This and following quotations are from *The Buried Life* by Matthew Arnold.

of air, the breeze, the fragrance, the forming and re-forming of the clouds and the vibrancy of the hills and valleys: they speak to you in whispers, but so does the reflected image within you; *feeling stirs*. The inner landscape also reveals its forms, colours and movement: 'the eye sinks inward and the heart lies plain'. You want to say: 'Do not ask me to speak, be silent around me, let me have my inner communion with what I am contemplating. I will not tell you because I cannot and I have no wish to. It is so new to me, that it must remain silently mine.'

Maturity is growing through the quickening of this feeling component of soul life. Feeling is not the same as 'the feelings' which belong to the emotional life. Feeling is that Cinderella between the two demanding sisters, Thinking and Willing. It can hardly be put into concepts: it calls for poetry, music or art to reveal to some degree the outer shell of what is experienced deep down. It is only rarely that the inmost heart is able to come to expression:

> Ah, well for us, if even we,
> Even for a moment, can get free
> Our heart, and have our lips unchained:
> For that which seals them has been deep-ordained.

It is too early to speak of love in the fifteen-year-old, but certainly the heart is preparing for it. This can give rise to inner tension: feeling wanting to expand and find expression, while the thinking arouses restricting self-consciousness. When the two work together the young person may show remarkable insight and understanding of others. This can cause him pain while his intellect can perceive, his feeling may turn that perception inward, and then he suffers when he sees others suffer. For instance he will agonize if he senses conflict in the relationship of his parents to each other. It is the birth of compassion.

Yet because of his newly experienced sensitivity he may cover up what he feels with brashness, even harshness. Home can become for him a place of acute embarrassment: it confines him, holds him in patterns which do not correspond with the daydreams that fill and expand his growing imagination. He will withdraw into his room when he needs a place to be safely on his own, or he will spend more time at school engaged in a variety of extra activities, if his school is enlightened enough to offer them. He has to make quite sure that his mother really and finally recognizes that he is no longer a kid. He dreams of being far away, but knows that he is not ready to leave the protection of home and parents. Not only is his imagination newly active: he has a longing, even a need, to *be* active. He can communicate best through doing something with someone else who is also absorbed in the same object of interest. This is easier for him than to sit talking face to face with another person, especially if that person is one of his parents.

Both boys and girls will want to spend time with the crowd, and the thrill of breaking new ground will lead occasionally to getting drunk at parties. A certain amount of sexual experiment will be started. What happens and how far it goes depends on various things, for instance boredom, or the influence of older teenagers or the impact of passive entertainment. Parents can probably sense when this is happening. It is good when such experiences can be spoken about; older sisters are best placed to be the confidantes of fifteen-year-old girls and can do most to help them not to run risks.

Boredom can be a problem at this in-between stage, when nothing seems worth doing. This phase (for it will pass) should not be seen just as slack behaviour or laziness. Of course it appears as this; but it goes deeper: the person is growing physically at a fast rate and much strength and inner stamina is drawn into this process. This phase of change is not easy to master: the ego is unable to penetrate the limbs, and the whole body is less easily organized. It takes a while before the altering *Gestalt* is mastered by the internal guiding force of the ego. It is quite difficult to 'get oneself going', because with the lack of initiative goes a good deal of moodiness. Music with a heavy beat (and a languid soul content) helps to absorb something of the malaise of this time of transition. But it does tend to become an addiction.

Parents must not reckon that fifteen will be easygoing!

It can happen that communication with parents or those in charge becomes so difficult that a longing to break out becomes irresistible. This can take the form of bad behaviour, defiance and even absconding. We had the experience of our eldest daughter at fifteen running away from the school hostel where she was living. Together with another girl, not even her best friend, she was gone: we had no idea where. After an anxious day-and-a-half, the police phoned us from a place seven hundred kilometres away. Friends of ours offered to collect her because just then our young son had to go into hospital for an osteitis operation. She returned, and we welcomed her back: no great scenes one way or the other. Gradually she told us all that had happened, including the two chilly nights in the police cell. Years later she said that the hardest thing for her was that she had caused us this anxiety just when we were worried about her brother's operation. We could then tell her about our acute anxiety at the time, but also our trust in her guardian angel. This breaking out was typical of fifteen: at times there must be a drama; this can be inconsiderate and constitute bad behaviour or cause enormous worry. When it happens it is earnestly meant, but later the young person will wince and smile at the foolhardiness that he or she displayed. Our daughter's excursion was a gesture of emancipation, and she did not have to repeat it. Independence is the aim, but initially it hurts.

Parents need to be sufficiently in touch to know when it is time to intervene and to establish limits. These limits must be consistently applied, to give the young person security. The inner battle between attachment and detachment makes for inner confusion, and this becomes worse if there are no parameters to give this security. The struggle at this age does lead to a refining of self-awareness. It is a maturing process, entailing a good deal of chaos. The inner tension between thinking (that gives rise to self-criticism) and feeling (that makes one vulnerable) causes a certain confusion which in school can result in a drop in performance and a deterioration in discipline. This may disappoint the teacher. The drop in performance may be only temporary, and due to this inner tension, which may be eased if the teacher can keep alive the interest of the pupil; or else it may indicate that something is happening in the life of the young person that needs investigation. An experienced teacher, in consultation with the parents, will be able to discern which it is.

Fifteen is not the age group most beloved by teachers! And yet young people will find comfort and support from school if the subjects can be embraced as *new learning* which evokes interest in the world. At the same time the young person needs to become involved with moral and ethical issues that present themselves to him through the subject matter. If this can come about, then the hunger for *meaning* is fed and the will of the pupils becomes positively engaged. If this does not happen, the pupils themselves may become fed up with school and seek ways of dropping out. And those who drop out may be just the ones who most needed meaningful teaching.

What presents itself to the young person's feeling life can be wonderful or dreadful. He or she begins to encounter darkness as well as light, and is exposed to unpleasantness to which the reaction may be violent.

This is the age when he can break out and become delinquent. Sometimes self-criticism and sense of failure turn the young person against his surroundings. When, as a child, he has been deprived of love, he will use his emerging independence to demonstrate to the world around him that he has no need for softness. He rejects the very gentleness of feeling that would stir within him. He cannot bear the fact that he might be dropping his defences against the world which he feels has no time for him. His problem is that he cannot trust kindness shown to him by others. Any proffered kindness is submitted to severe testing to ensure that it is genuine. The tests are not easy to withstand: the maladjusted or deprived young person can be very tough, and his testing can be survived only by someone who can 'see the person' beyond the difficult behaviour and can meet him positively. If the young person feels this regard, he may begin to trust the one who is recognizing him in this way, and this trust may develop into trusting others as well, and so build up his openness towards a world which he thought he had to fight.

Basic trust in people is a great help to a teenager traversing fifteen. This needs to have been established in the very early phase of life and to have been nurtured throughout childhood. The test then comes at this age, when the young person begins to be more sensitive and unsure. If he feels secure enough to listen to all that stirs in his own soul, this listening can be deep, and reveal to him the mysteries of beauty and love. The buried Self becomes discernible for the first time. For a while such feelings must be kept within himself: they cannot face the daylight. The person is tender, and so needs an armour. No one should try and pierce the armour, because to do so can cause a wound that could take years and years to heal, if it heals at all.

Sixteen

Whilst at fifteen the adolescent has to claim that he or she is no longer a child, at sixteen the battle for recognition of one's growing up generally comes to an end quite soon: parents, teachers and other grown-up persons accord the sixteen-year-old an instinctive respect. There is a personality, indeed a person, to be met, whom one meets readily. Parents begin to find it quite reasonable to relate to their sixteen-year-old as an equal-in-the-making: the parent-child relationship moves for precious moments into an adult-adult one. This comes about because the touchy sensitive infirmness of fifteen transforms at sixteen into a more ordered, self-reliant and outgoing self-assurance.

This is the ideal picture, especially when the 'precious moments' become frequent and regular. The sixteen-year-old begins to transform that inner sensitivity which he experienced at fifteen into an outreach towards people in general, thanks to a dropping of barriers. It is good if this can include those close to him, but it can happen that they are just the ones who most tend to see him as he was and not as he is. We tend to form mental pictures of each other, which are not always flexible enough to keep up with the rapidly-changing sixteen-year-old. This can make him feel hemmed in, just when he wishes to be seen freshly as he now is (which will be different in three months' time). So there could be a certain amount of vacillation on the part of parents, who at times treat their sixteen-year-old as becoming an 'equal' to themselves, and at others find it difficult to keep up with the rapid changes.

The right of another person to be as he or she is can now be accepted, because the young person himself wants to be accepted by others as he is. Moreover, tolerance will grow to the extent that the teenager is able to accept himself. The feeling of moving through, developing and yet not being quite there is engendered by the experience of strong forces of growth.

The inwardness of feeling that showed itself dramatically at fifteen is now not so self-absorbing: a certain sensitivity still remains, but this now shows as a new openness and an ability to look outward. The sixteen-person is more interested in others, more aware of them, and more tolerant: less and less does he want to be 'one up' with mocking or clever remarks. The power of judgment has grown more balanced and there is a greater awareness of the wide span of possibility of choice: so it becomes understandable that others may choose differently from oneself. This is a major breakthrough in terms of a growing feeling for what is social. Moreover, when the sixteen-year-old realizes the many choices facing him, he also begins to wake up to the consequences that he will have to live with if he makes the wrong choice. He will find himself gradually building up some kind of value system. Whilst experiments have to be made for the sake of experience, the young person can begin to foresee what would happen to him or her if a certain course is pursued. The son or daughter likes to tell the parents: 'Don't worry; I'll be all right,' and realizes that this means:

'Whatever I do, I'll have to pick up the bits myself and maybe carry them for the rest of my life: so I'll watch out; otherwise I shall have only myself to blame.'

The sixteen-person becomes able to grasp that a supposed enjoyment now may not be worthwhile if it cuts out a greater and more real advantage later. He will have to come to terms with smoking, alcohol, sex and the taking of drugs of various kinds (beginning with 'only occasionally' and the 'mild harmless' ones). Keen observation of the way these four enticements have become addictions in older people can strengthen the resolve to handle them with care. This will be the more evident if the young person realizes that he will need his faculties for working, even if he is not yet clear what his future will be.

If he leaves school, it is a hard blow if he faces unemployment at the outset. If the young person is not to go into further education, everything possible should be done by parents, teachers and counsellors to enable him to get into work and 'make it'. It is a time of energetic optimism and will, and of flowing self-assurance, which engenders the forming of ideals and aims.

Alongside the growing maturity there is growth in intellect. At sixteen comes the high point of intellectual ability: it is the time of glory in thinking. This it is that commands the respect of those around. Parents are impressed (even shown up) and teachers gratified (or challenged). And with this goes a greater self-control in the sphere of the emotions. Anger, moodiness and impulsiveness feature less in the general behaviour, and there is less restlessness than during the fifteen-year. He will try to earn money through jobs in the holidays, and so move out of the accustomed borders of family, school and local community.

Both boys and girls have by now little more physical growing to do and have become somewhat settled in their sexual identity.

There is the gripping enjoyment of rhythm and beat, which releases (or maybe stimulates) bodily tensions. There is a fund of energy to use up, and music and dancing counterbalance the demands of concentrated school work. Young people of this age spend much of their time in the company of their contemporaries, but do not succumb so easily to group pressures. Though identification with the group will still be strong, there will be more detachment from pressure to conform: they begin to appreciate the feeling of freedom from such pressure.

Seventeen

With seventeen one can actually say that adolescence is in full swing. The years of puberty are over, and indeed the person is 'becoming an adult'. 'Becoming' implies an inner tension between 'what I am' and 'what I am to become'. At this stage the young person's whole motivation is directed forward. Schooling is drawing to an end, and the time is coming when he or she will leave the nest of the family; this time may already have come.

The school leaver who now becomes a wage earner finds himself plunged into an adult world without being fully ready for it: from being at the senior end of his school, he will find himself all too abruptly a junior in the vast workforce of employed people. The school curriculum was varied: now (especially if he has a job in a factory) he may find that working life is repetitive, consisting of unchallenging and boring operations which do little for his feeling of self-worth or for the fulfilment of ideals that have begun to stir in him. Worse still is when there is no job for him; *he isn't needed:* he is superfluous to society and cannot yet become a contributor at home. A crushing sense of defeat can arise, a feeling of cynicism which drives the young person into groups and gangs that turn against the unsatisfying order to which he belongs but which does not receive him.

If he has remained at school, he will be working towards his school-leaving exams. This is no problem if he can find the subject matter meaningful: but there is the risk that the subject matter itself will lose its appeal if it now becomes a means to an end. If the only aim is to get through the examination, it hardly seems to matter whether the pupil is interested in what he is learning. When creativity in the school programme has to be sacrificed for the sake of exams, this can be a grey period: to be endured and lived through. The sole consolation is the shining light that beckons towards freedom at the end of the tunnel.

A happy seventeen-year-old, at school or already out at work, can say quietly to himself: 'I don't look for authority in those around me or in what I am learning. I look for it in myself.' For then he will find that something new is beginning to stir in him. For moments, flashes of insight may light up a much wider horizon than he ever dreamt was possible; he will be experiencing his own spirit. At this point these will be only glimpses of a revelation that will grow in the coming years. He will find himself thinking: 'The world is greater, deeper and more wonderful than I had ever imagined' .

This joyful expansion can be the result of a new experience that can overtake the young man or woman, the experience of *falling in love.* It is one of the sad things about our present culture that we use the word 'erotic' to

describe the prompting of sexuality. Eros has little to do
with sex as such. It is a quite different force that stirs in
the soul: namely one that sees in someone of the opposite sex an ideal that causes one's own sun to rise and
shine with warmth and light, in devotion to the one who
glows in one's feeling. The object of love may be
remote, untouchable, as with the Troubadours: they sang
of the beauty, virtue and goodness living in the lady
whom they knew would never be theirs. And when a girl
is lost in admiration for a man, maybe she sees him only
as an image of an ideal and does not know him in reality. Eros is romantic love, delight in contemplating the
qualities that one attributes to that person, an exciting
infatuation which invades one's consciousness by day
and one's dreams at night. Eros is the glorious regard for
someone else: and yet it is at the same time the discovery of an ideal in one's own self. The mystery of man
and woman, and how one presents the ideal for the
other, can become a new experience for the adolescent
person. It is a negative element in modern culture that
the romantic ideal is quickly associated with the stirring
of sexuality and the fulfilment of love seen in physical
terms.

The physical aspect of love is not in itself sinful or
degrading. The body is full of wisdom and goodness, so
that intimacy with someone of the opposite sex can be
profoundly satisfying: it calls up a mood of giving and
receiving: such is the ideal; it reveals the wonder of the
'other'. This helps to affirm the sexual identity of each,
which is a vital confirmation of oneself. What can go
wrong is that the instinctive drive of sexuality can overwhelm the caring sensitivity and push the couple into an
involvement with each other which threatens the inner
freedom of both. The effect can be wounding, hurting and

permanently damaging to the being of both, but especially of the woman. We will delve further into the awakening of sexuality later.

Against this background of expanding horizons and deepening experiences the young person comes to the moment when a decision has to be made about training and work. His soul experiences the width of the world around him, but active entry into this world demands a narrowing-down. This stirs the question: 'What am I capable of doing?' — and makes one look at one's own gifts and limitations. Through this inner dialogue with oneself one may begin to discern one's own destiny and the course of life one will want to follow. As this realization becomes clearer, one may ask the question: 'What do I want to do with my life?'

So at seventeen life becomes more serious. Adulthood and its responsibilities are beginning to dawn. How to move on to the next phase of life? The young person begins to realize that everything depends on the marshalling of his own will-forces; he may be stimulated by other people and by the institutions around him, but if he is to be free he has to become master of his own will, independent of props. The restraints of school and family may still have to be accepted for a while, but the time for leaving the cocoon and spreading his wings is approaching fast.

Eighteen

Eighteen brings a time of great significance. This was recognized in the ancient mystery centres: it was the age when important steps were taken towards initiation. This had to do with opening the soul, consciously, to two mysterious phenomena which were to become part of the young person's experience: love and life.

Greek mythology shows this dynamic in the story of Persephone and Pluto. It can be found in one of the very earliest of all plays, 'The Sacred Drama of Eleusis': this formed part of the initiation ceremonies of young Greeks on the brink of adulthood. Persephone is the 'teenage' daughter of Demeter. She is playing peacefully with her friends in the meadows of Eleusis. Suddenly, through a plot of Pluto, she is taken hold of and dragged down through a cave into the underworld, and there presented as captive to Pluto, the god of Hades. Pluto desires to possess her and make her his queen, but first she must forget all that connects her with the world of life: she must drink the juice of the pomegranate, which will blot out all her memories and make her amenable to becoming Queen of the Dead. Ghostly beings frighten her. Souls of the dead held captive by Pluto plead with her to lead them back to the light, away from the dim gloom where they find themselves tormented by terrible apparitions: they are afraid they will never escape from this frightful prison.

Persephone is faced with the brute power of Pluto and his drive to possess her. He urges her to drink from the cup; to begin with she resists, but gradually she becomes enticed by the dark red potion. There stirs in her a fascination for her monstrous captor. She lifts the cup to her lips, now no longer rejecting it but wanting it ... Meanwhile the mother-love of Demeter has been at work to rescue her. Demeter has found Triptolemos of Eleusis, a courageous young prince who would rather work on the soil than inherit his father's crown. His father has just died, and the citizens are about to assemble in the market-place to proclaim a new king. Rejecting the chance of kingship, Triptolemos meets Demeter, at first disguised as an old widow who is sorrowing over the loss of her daughter. When he hears her story he takes pity on her and is prepared for any adventure that would restore her daughter to her. Demeter, helped by the witch-like goddess Hecate, prepares him to break through the gates of Hades. Triptolemos bursts into Pluto's underworld in the instant that Persephone lifts the potion to her lips. He calls out to her to remember her true home, and she drops the cup, the drink untouched. Pluto is furious but powerless; Triptolemos leads Persephone out of Hades.

Through this drama the young candidates were confronted with the mysteries of life and love. Persephone nearly lost her life by being caught in the world of the dead, and she nearly became enslaved by passion masquerading as love. The feeling for life and for love grows stronger if it is realized through a shock or a sudden loss that both are precarious. Yet both seem to call for risk taking: 'Nothing ventured, nothing gained'. The possibility of losing one or other of them, or a foretaste of so doing, makes one value them much more consciously. But there is the need to *challenge* life and to *venture* in the field of love. This is the time of involvement in sports which bring experiences that overreach the safety of ordinary existence, like hang-gliding, scuba-diving, mountain climbing, sailing or advanced showjumping. The person pits himself or herself against the elements and seeks adventure that stretches his or her physical and mental agility to the utmost. It is a challenge to discover one's potential; to test one's courage, nimbleness and power of decision in adverse circumstances, and so become aware of limitations. All this so as to achieve *more* from oneself. It serves to awaken spiritual capacities.

Even if adventure is not actively sought, crises can occur which test the courage and tenacity of the young person.

The innocent Persephone is taken off to Hades by Pluto's plot: in many subtle and devious ways the young person may be dragged off into unfreedom by addictions of various kinds and have to face dangerous consequences. Dramatic can be the encounters with despair and a sense of powerlessness and hopelessness, suicide presenting a tempting way out. This is something that has to be reckoned with by those around. Talk of suicide has to be taken seriously: but it is helpful to know that what presents itself as a death-wish is at this stage invariably a life-wish, which contains the incisive question: 'Does anyone care about me?'

Young Greeks who went to the Mystery school of Eleusis had to experience the drama working deeply into themselves. Then they were led into a hall resplendent with light, where the figure of Demeter shone before them: Demeter, the goddess of abundant life and caring love.

Life and love: What makes one aware of them is the vibrant tension in each. There spring up within a person the questions 'How does love work?' and 'What is life for?' 'Where is their truth?' 'What is their meaning?' Life is there to be engaged upon; love overtakes one and brings a network of feelings and emotions, often self-contradictory, and then demands one's devoted and constant care.

There are a number of countries that require the young men of eighteen to undergo a period of military training. From the moment they first handle a rifle, they are taught to regard 'the enemy' as destructible. It is their task to bring about the loss of human life: the purpose is clearly to *kill.* This counters the ideals of reverence for life and the worth of the human being, which begin to form in young people being touched by the grandeur of life and love. The 'sixties' generation brought the message 'make love, not war'. Since then there has grown in the world an awareness of how nuclear conflict could escalate into the utter destruction of humanity. Many young people cannot accept that it is necessary to play with guns. They cannot accept the need to fight for nationalistic or racial purposes. They have no connection to conflict prompted by political or economic motivation. They cannot support the protection of an unjust establishment. Why should they be involved in such military action? Where an alternative peace service is not allowed, such young men are placed in an impossible personal conflict.

The age of eighteen is indeed often accompanied by an upsurge of genuine spiritual feeling. The ideals of the spiritual life lead young people to seek a philosophy and an ethic which satisfies their search for the meaning of *life*. It is the age when a young person wants to find some way to serve ideals, and so may think about becoming a monk or a nun, or will seek a career of service to the cause of peace, ecology, or of helping handicapped or disadvantaged people. These aims may be felt passionately and be accompanied by eloquent criticism of the established order.

The power of love leads the young person into another realm of experience. Love hits the person personally: no one else can have the same experience. However it may appear to others, even to the beloved, only the person in whom love has stirred knows how deep it goes and how all-consuming and demanding the feeling is. Through love there will come pain. The great magical expansion of the soul, filling it with delight and unbounded hope and calling up visions of what could be, exposes the soul to bitter disappointment or a feeling of numb powerlessness if the expectations prove unfounded. When the object of the ecstatic love proves unworthy, or unable to receive such adulation, a painful collapse ensues; then, with broken heart, the young person turns inward. He may be fortunate enough to see that his love was not really directed at the beloved, but was a discovery of his own ideal. Falling in love is often a sudden awareness of one's own spirit. A glimpse is afforded of the pure, radiant and beautiful part of one's Self, which one projects or ascribes to the person who stirred the new experience.

True love for another person is different from this sudden explosion of romantic delight: it is born of giving a place in one's heart to that person, and leaving him or her free to come in or go out at will. Any constraint, demand or even emotional dependence is a sign that the love is not selfless, and therefore not true. Spiritual love is a high ideal, but only this kind of love is *Agape,* the love spoken of in the Gospels. The romantic love is Eros, and this, with its worshipping of the beloved, is pursued more for what it gives to oneself than for what it gives to another. Between these two forms of love is a middle one, called in Greek *Philia.* Philia is the love that stabilizes and enriches human relationships with friendly affection. Through Philia we enjoy one another, accompany each other through stresses and difficulties, and celebrate each other's achievements. This is the form of love that brings peace. It is free of the group bonding of adolescent boys, and of the intensive one-to-one relationship of adolescent girls, both of which are more like a dependency. It is neither the ideal selfless Agape of the fully mature, spiritually centred adult, nor is it the strong romantic dream of young Eros. And above all it is not the driving force of sexuality. The growth of Philia in the hearts of young people is a sign of adulthood being near.

So eighteen is a decisive time. In many countries the person is given the vote and is treated by law as no longer a minor. The person may seem ready outwardly, but he is not quite ready inwardly: the Ego or Spirit is not in full control, and there are still areas of immaturity. This requires the completion of the third seven-year-cycle and explains why twenty-one has been more rightly chosen as the age at which full responsibility can be assumed. So whilst the person may be well endowed by the end of his eighteen years, he still has to reach the mooring which will mean for him full independence at twenty-one. For it is only then that he will be able to look back at the expanse of the sea through which he has sailed, and look forward towards the land of adulthood.

Nineteen

At nineteen the person needs to prove his freedom. Not just a freedom of choice or a freedom from outer restraints, but a freedom to create and to shape his or her life. This freedom implies the achievement of practical skills and life-skills. He must be capable of work, but also of responding to all the needs and demands that come towards him. By recognizing his limitations he will be able to know where he can help himself and where he must ask for help. Knowing limits and accepting them is a sign of maturity. He will want to put himself to the test. For this a new and unpredictable set of experiences is needed. He must travel. Either geographically or spiritually, preferably both. He may engage in a spiritual journey in search of his own philosophy of life. He may set out on an actual journey with little money, prepared to rough it with just a backpack, ready to sleep in the hills or on station platforms in distant countries, meeting his peers of many other nations and cultures. He will get to know what it is like to be poor, hungry and alone. He will learn the value of companionship, the sharing of the bread. He will start to become street-wise: to know the darker, sadder, more desolate sides of life; to see how poor people live in locations, slums and shanty-towns; to meet the power of wealth which gives rise to privilege; and gradually to realize that happiness is born in serving others and in serving one's ideals. Through this he comes to the meaning of life. All is summed up by the phrase 'meeting reality'.

But the 'real' may indeed be only the outer shell of reality: he has still to penetrate the deeper, less transient and more significant reality that is beyond time and space, the eternal behind all appearance. For this quest he has the next phases of life. Now it is the everyday reality that he has to meet and handle. This reality begins to confront him with barriers, and he will have many collisions with blocks on his path. His maturity will be tested in the way that he reacts: whether he turns back, or whether he strives to remove the blocks in whatever way may be possible for him. He must know his limitations and how to set about reducing them.

His feelings and thoughts may be youthfully extreme: he may feel passionately about the causes that he embraces; he may find that others consider him not quite in touch with 'reality' as they see it. But his passionate conviction reveals a furnace of heart-fire which will smelt the rough ore in his soul and bring out the purified metal. This is no time for low profiles and coolly-held intellectual propositions. The person at the end of his or her teen years faces the ailing condition of mankind. Will the ailment engulf him and make him part of itself? Or can he be inwardly free enough to work out of his own centre and prepare himself to play his part in raising the condition of Man? Whatever his aim, he will need to know that there are people who believe in him and respect his ideals.

Each new rising generation brings new hope, just as each age has its special problems. With knowledge and conviction, and a heart that has courage, the young person can make a difference. Much depends on how he has grown during the teen years, what influences have worked on him and how he has felt within himself. Important will be the degree of inner freedom that has grown in him, the freedom to be creative and to persevere against opposing odds.

6. Landmarks on the way

Rhythms in biography

Studies in the development of a person reveal a rhythmic succession of turning points. They form the pattern on which the biography is structured. Two important rhythms are the seven-year periods and the moon nodes. Each seven years marks a major development phase. At *seven* the teeth change, signifying that life-forces have completed the initial building-up of the body and some can now be 'spared' for learning: hence it is time for school. The *fourteen-year* 'threshold' signifies puberty and the transition from childhood to youth. At fourteen the physical development achieves ripeness of the reproductive functions, and the soul begins its expansion of interest in the world. The innate seeds of morality, interest and judgment begin to germinate in the soul to enable it to fulfil the demands of earthly existence. At *twenty-one* the Self is born and the person enters adulthood. (We shall go into this in the next chapter.) As the *twenty-eighth* year approaches there is a further change, though it is not always so noticeable.

The moon nodes come roughly every eighteen-and-a-half years, and mark the times in life when major changes can take place. The first of these and the fourteen-year transition fall into the teen years, and both will be surveyed in this chapter.

Transition at fourteen

The teen years, as we have seen, are a time of rapid development and change, during which the growing person has to draw his strength not only from his parents and teachers, but from 'inner' sources as well: his own individuality is gradually released from a kind of motherly sheath and begins to unfold, like a bud that opens in springtime. Indeed it is the spring of the individual person.

What shapes his soul is more than what he inherited from his parents, more than the influence of his environment. There are other areas from which he can now draw: from his own inborn soul-forces, from the working of destiny, from the divine world, and even from the dark counter forces that begin to have free play at this stage. These various influences make up the amazing dynamic of the teen years and carry on through the rest of life.

We shall describe these influences, which are in constant interplay. It is difficult to draw clear boundaries between them, but it is helpful to identify them because of their effect on the person.

There is indeed the influence of *heredity:* what he has received from his parents.

Also the formative impact of his *environment:* the house, street, town and country in which he has grown up, the first language that he learned, his position among his brothers and sisters, and much else besides.

There is his own *constitution,* not only his bodily make-up but also the natural forces of his soul, from unconscious drives and instincts to the more refined and conscious powers of thinking, feeling and will. Included here is his temperament: everything, in fact, that makes up his 'personality'. This does, in part, have to do with heredity and environment, but by no means entirely: think how different siblings are from each other.

Then there is *destiny.* It may be over-simplifying, but one can say that destiny stems from the past and gradually reveals itself. It consists of the 'karma' a person brings with him and his personal mission in life. The mission is affected by the karma, but the two are not identical. Both will show themselves through the pattern of events in the biography of the person.

There is *divine grace,* the direct working of the spiritual world, resulting from the relationship to God, whether or not this is conscious. It includes the work of the guardian angel, as messenger of the divine.

And there are the *opposing forces.* A person's own freedom subsists in the fact that he can do wrong. There are negative spiritual entities working in the world that would lead him away from his own true course. By developing his resistance to these forces and acquiring mastery over them he strengthens his ego.

The ego has to work with or confront all these influences and forces. This ego begins to be free to develop itself at puberty and is 'born' at twenty-one; its task is to be the 'organizer': synthesizing and directing all the energies and influences, and bringing about the individualization of the person. The ego is not ready for this tremendous task, as it is still only in the developing stage. Yet, immature as it is, it involves itself in the process, which can go smoothly only if it can accept a kind of apprenticeship status for its new task; this means recognizing its need to learn and being content to wait for full responsibility. But usually the ego cannot accept this: the parents are no longer permitted to give the guidance and support that they could properly give in childhood. The young person himself, although still so unequipped, has to cope with all that comes towards him as his potential unfolds, and to meet with the counter-forces that threaten him on either side. The parents are needed as much as ever, but their role is different now.

The influences of heredity and environment, the growing personality, the divine working and the opposing forces are interrelated in various ways. Some people would say that all are varying aspects of the person's destiny; others that he is in the hands of God and everything happens under His immediate guidance. It can also be said that the pattern of behaviour is conditioned or modified by environment. What is presented here is the idea that each force should be seen in its own right as part of a highly complex interweaving that begins to work on the young person when he reaches fourteen.

We shall not dwell long on the hereditary and environmental, as these are well researched.'* It is one of the insights of spiritual science that the soul preparing for a life on earth seeks out the parents who can provide it with a right initial environment as well as with the bodily and soul constitution suitable for the fulfilling of its destiny. These are vital factors in life and do not happen by accident.

Destiny as karma and mission

It would go too far to consider the significance of the horoscope: to speak of the characteristics that have to do with our birth sign and the imprint of the heavens at the moment of our birth. We want here to focus attention more generally on the circumstances that come to meet us. Nothing occurs by chance: our meetings with others and the events of our biography are all part of the

* As in *Phases of Childhood* by Bernard Lievegoed (Floris Books 1987).

unfolding of our *destiny*. This does not mean that we are subjugated by these events: it is up to us to meet them consciously and in freedom, with the strength of our ego. The knowledge of reincarnation and karma, which forms an important element in contemporary spiritual science, enables us to understand why brothers and sisters often have such different lives. It can happen in a family that one child sails through adolescence with calm waters and light winds, success in school and friendships and a clear feeling about which career to follow, while a brother or sister may struggle at every point and fail.

According to the law of karma, debts must be paid and wrongs righted: one faces the need to complete unfinished work from a previous life. Yet we don't come to earth only with karma. There is more: we also have a mission. The earth-life that confronts us at birth is not merely conditioned from the past, even though the past is woven into it, for the scene is new. Also the task that faces us is new. *A special mission waits for each of us,* and before coming to earth we may well have *agreed* to take on this particular mission: this means we have had a part in writing the script of our biography.

Our own involvement in the scriptwriting may have even presented a further possibility: we may have offered to take on some part of the karmic debt of another person if we have not had too many karmic obligations of our own; even to take on something of the karma of the world. To take on karma that is not one's own is a deed of love. Those who are born with a mental or physical handicap may not be having to work out their own karma, but may be carrying the karma of others: such is the feeling of many who have worked among handicapped people and have come to know such destinies.

After Jesus has healed the man born blind, as recorded in the Gospel of John, the disciples wonder at his being *born* blind and ask Jesus whether the man is carrying the karma of his parents or his own (which can only refer to a previous life):

> And his disciples asked him
>> Rabbi
>> Was it he or his parents who sinned
>> Causing him to be born blind?

But Jesus answers that there is a higher purpose not connected with his own personal karma, namely that the works of God be made manifest:

> Jesus answered
>> Neither he nor his parents have sinned
>> It is so
>> That the deeds of God within him
>> May appear outwardly*

So the other side to destiny is one's mission in life. Each soul born on earth confronts a task which goes beyond his own karma. There will be the unfolding of his gifts, his sensing of a vocation, and the events and meetings which guide him along a particular path. When parents and others believe that a growing person has his own mission, even if they have no perception of what it is, the young person will be helped to discern it for himself. In Chapter Five we spoke of how the person of seventeen needs to ask the question: 'What am I capable of doing?' We saw there that it was too early to ask the question:

* John 9:2f, rendering by Kalmia Bittleston (Floris Books 1984)

'What does life want from me?' What is relevant in the teen years is the reality of this mission in life, which can gradually become self-evident to the young person, particularly if he is supported and encouraged by those close to him.

How does the life-task connect with karma? This question is difficult to answer because for each person it is different. In general karma provides the 'given' whilst the mission belongs to the creative response to what is given. I may be handicapped in this or that way because that is my karma, but it may be my mission to bring a group of people together to set up a whole system of support for persons with a like handicap; or to become a spokesman for other afflicted people, with the task of opening the hearts of all who come in reach. Helen Keller's fateful illness in her second year consigned her to a dark and silent world: but Anne Sullivan was waiting for the life-task that came her way, and Helen found the means to transform her handicap into a blessing for many.

A person can deny or ignore his mission; we are surrounded by instances of people failing to take up their mission in life, wasting opportunities and denying their potential, to say nothing of irresponsibly making themselves unfit for doing what their mission asks of them. Our mission will remain hidden from us as long as we reject our life-situation. Once we can accept and trust ourselves and our situation, the meaning of our life can begin to show itself. This may have to start quite simply with saying: 'Maybe I should stop grumbling and accept what is.' This would be a beginning, and from there we may be able to go further and realize other advantages that have come our way because of what has happened to us in our life. With this we are on the track of discovering that nothing really comes about by chance, and from there we can go further and recognize that life isn't a meaningless succession of events that mostly don't go the way we want them to go. We begin instead to realize that just those everyday events can lead us the right way if we respond to them with an open heart. The open heart can work magnetically to bring new situations into our life, and gradually set us on the course that is really ours.

At the fourteen-year turning point this process begins to unfold. Such considerations may help parents to look for the meaning in all that they encounter in the dynamism of daily living with their teenagers. Moreover, it can help parents to recognize that their sons or daughters have their own way to go, and they should not feel themselves responsible for all that happens.

Grace

The story of the man born blind can make us aware that whilst there is personal destiny there can also be *divine intervention*. One can say that it was the blind man's karma to meet the Christ and be healed, but there is a further dimension: namely that a miracle took place. Divine light flowed into the life of this man who had lived in darkness till this moment of healing. One can recall words from many scriptures that show that the divine love is an inborn fact which has nevertheless to be discovered by each person. In the Old Testament, at the beginning of the Book of Jeremiah (1:4f NEB) there stands: 'The Word of the Lord came to me: "Before I formed you in the womb I knew you for my own; before you were born I consecrated you".' In the Gospel of John, Christ, in praying to the Father, speaks the words:

I in them
And thou in me
So that they may be completely one
And the world may be aware
That thou hast sent me out
And hast loved them
As thou hast loved me.*

The divine is working through all the other factors that affect our lives, in that it works in the very force of life itself. We can say that there is a higher power that stands over and above all that conditions us through heredity, environment and destiny. This is grace. There can be dramatic events which cause us to say 'a miracle has happened', as when a person is saved at the last moment from drowning, or averts involvement in a serious accident. There are many far less impressive events which are equally graced in the everyday life of a person when, in the face of need or difficulty, he opens his heart to the divine, or when someone else intercedes on his behalf. We can seek grace through the activity of our inner life, through the openness to inspiration that comes with meditation and prayer And there is the possibility of bringing an inflow of special grace through sacramental rites: the baptizing of a baby, the confirming of an adolescent, the blessing of a couple seeking community of life in marriage, and the anointing of a person approaching death. There can be communion with the redeeming and healing powers that work through the being of Christ. Our deeds of selfless love towards others create a climate in which grace can flow. A blow of destiny, suffering and illness, an enormous disappointment: all these are hard to bear, but

* 17:23 rendering by Kalmia Bittleston

they can make us open to the flow of grace. We may have to be totally emptied out, or brought to the lowest ebb of our self-esteem or our physical strength (like the prodigal son) before this happens. Destiny needs to play taskmaster until we have achieved our freedom: it has to grip us until *we* can grip *it*. Jacob (Genesis 32) had to wrestle with the angel before he could be given his true name. We may also have to go through a struggle in order to become our own master.

Each person has his link with the divine world through his own *angel*. The angel is the messenger who weaves between the divine world and the individual who is on earth. The young person may gradually become conscious that he has his guardian. There is a mysterious relationship between each person and the being of the angelic world who guides him and remains his companion throughout his incarnations. There are times when a person can have a tangible experience of his angel, as when he is in extreme danger and God works through the angel to help him.

This relationship can be cultivated and become more and more felt. When one goes to sleep at the end of the day, the ego meets the angel and together they *re-view* all that has happened during the day. This enables the experiences to be transformed into fruits to be offered back to the divine world. Through this review the person develops an understanding for things that had perplexed him, and this will strengthen his moral impulses for dealing with his everyday life. Through his growing sensitivity he can become more conscious by day of the effect of these meetings at night. There are times when, for the sake of the maturing of the individual, the angel will stand back, and this explains why there are periods when one feels bereft and left to one's own devices: this is particularly so at the threshold of the twenty-eighth year. So the angel is also like a good educator, knowing when to be close and when to be more withdrawn. The angels cannot fully experience what we experience on earth because they have no physical body and lack the consciousness that we have through being incarnated: hence it is important that we communicate with our angel, through inner conversation or prayer.

The soul of an all-round healthy child is open to his angel. But deadening education, unnatural food and bombardment of the senses through television and other sound and visual media join forces to threaten this innate sensitivity. When a child reaches adolescence, his growing intellect, combined with other elements, can have the effect of closing off that sensitive part of his soul. This renders the angel less able to give effective guidance, yet the angel remains with the person, thus giving opportunity for the gradual awakening of his *deeper sensitivity*. It is just this sensitivity that can foster an increasing awareness of the companionship of his heavenly guardian. Those who help to heal the sensitivity in young people who are deadened or darkened can bring about a change in their whole disposition: they bring rain to parched land. A person who becomes sensitive to the effects of his nightly meeting with the angel will be able to discern the guidance that is coming to him. This will help him to become his own authentic self, not cramped by inflexible rules but guided by an on-going conversation with the being who leads him towards the fulfilment of his destiny. It will also lead him to a growing awareness of spiritual activity in himself and around him as he goes through life. In turn this strengthens the unfolding of the powers of judgment, interest and morality.

Opposing forces

There will be another set of influences that will enter, or try to enter, the soul of a teenager, now that parental protection is changing and leaving him more vulnerable. These are the *opposer-powers,* the Adversaries. The young person has to encounter the forces of evil. These will show themselves in two ways. Either constitutes a force that would lead the person into denial of his own true worth and the destruction of his freedom.

The first tries to draw him into an unreal world of fantasy: this is not dark but full of light, the kind of light that leads his consciousness away into a dream so that he is no longer able to distinguish truth from falsehood; he is enticed into the delights of the senses and loses his normal feeling of responsibility: his ability to be his own master is undermined and it is difficult for him to resist. This power may be called *Lucifer,* he who thinks himself equal to God, and sows the seeds of a deceiving false pride into our souls. Lucifer would like to prevent man from doing just what the adolescent is called upon to do: to *grow* up. It is Luciferic for him to want freedom before he can be responsible. Also to try to reach the 'spirit' without effort. Lucifer tempts us to avoid having to walk the hard road of inner development that leads to a conscious, ego-directed knowledge of the spiritual realm.

For example, hallucinatory drugs appear to widen the consciousness without one's own effort: but they have three harmful effects. They encourage the drug-taker to seek spiritual experiences that *bypass* consciousness instead of developing from it; they engender an experience that is false, based on hallucination rather than a true meeting with spiritual entities; and they weaken the will, riddling it with lacerations that never fully heal, thereby reducing the person's possibility of achieving mastery over his life-situation. The drug culture is one section of Lucifer's business: his allurements are strong and our freedom easily undermined. He has other ways to deflect the young person from acquiring his own egohood: tobacco and alcohol are also part of his enterprise.

Satan and *Ahriman* are names for the second opposer: he is active in the opposite direction from Lucifer. His pull is to the earth, that we forget the heavens: remember the pomegranate potion Pluto gave to Persephone? In Ahriman's conception of the world there is no space for a spiritual dimension: for a notion to be accepted it has to be proved scientifically in terms of known causes and effects. The nature of an illness, for instance, is to be explained in terms of the functions of the body: any attempt at a deeper, more spiritual explanation, say in terms of karma, is 'unscientific' and so has to be excluded. Ahriman cannot see the liveliness of nature in its dancing forms: stripped of its spiritual dimension it appears only as the chemistry of elements which achieve organic structures without a spiritual plan. And in human behaviour he cannot distinguish between deeds of hatred and deeds of love. He conjures up the view that man's thoughts and actions are impelled by outside stimuli: his behaviour pattern can be conditioned and manipulated from outside himself. Like this, man can no longer be responsible for his own conduct. Such a world-conception has no room for wisdom, whereas cleverness is highly regarded if it proves effective and brings results. Personal values become unimportant. In his drive for power over the human being, Ahriman brings about denial of the divine and a subtle or blatant destruction of personal freedom. He encourages us to want everything cut and dried, coldly efficient, square and dead-looking (like much architecture of the modernist style). Meanwhile he entertains us through the media, dulling our human capacities hypnotically, so that we do not realize that he is genially amusing us to death.

Unlike Lucifer, Ahriman hastens us forward: he hassles us on, faster and faster, urging us to use our intellect to construct heaven on earth by all manner of mechanical means. And the more our 'progress' outstrips our morality, our judgment and our compassion, the more he can put our ego-development at risk. When the adolescent feels the power of his own intellect expanding through the natural unfolding of his faculties, he is vulnerable to the enticement to become a *brain* to the exclusion of his *heart* (and much of the ordinary educational system supports him in this). Or, when he is developing his aims, he can be gripped by ambition for material goods.

In much of this Ahriman enlists Lucifer as a partner, but through his extraordinary cleverness he retains the whip hand. The thump of beat music amplified to deafening pitch in the disco, the subdued lights irradiated with strobe and other effects, make the young person open for subliminal suggestion that the world is an underworld with little meaning. So what's in it for him, except to get all he can (with Ahriman's help), or else escape into the dream world (set up by Lucifer)? We have described the negative effect of these opposing powers. But, through clarity and resolve, the young person can begin to harness these energies and tame the dragons. Indeed Lucifer and Ahriman can be helpful to us. Lucifer brings lightness and beauty into artistic endeavours. And Ahriman is to be acknowledged in the mechanical and technical equipment that facilitates our daily life. They have their parts to play, but the person must keep control, curbing the excesses. It is man's task to stand between Lucifer and Ahriman in full consciousness and hold the balance.

So while the young person has to reckon with these opposing forces, he can also become conscious of his own innate strength and the helping hand from the divine. These dynamics start to engage the teenager just at the time when teachers and parents have to stand back. They need to go on supporting the young person with under-standing and to lead him further into knowledge; they should remain available for guidance. But they also have to give him space to grow and learn experimentally about all these aspects of life.

Many religious bodies offer their teenage adherents a service of confirmation to celebrate the transition that has been reached. In these services the divine world is asked to grant the young person courage and inner firmness. In The Christian Community the preparation takes between one and two years, thus covering the onset of puberty and accompanying the young people through the physical and soul changes of this time. Confirmands are led into a knowledge of the New Testament, the Sacraments and the religious life in a way that provides them with spiritual substance from which they can draw for the rest of their lives. Confirmation, at fourteen, calls upon the Being of Christ to become a companion through joyful and sor-rowful times of life.

So fourteen is an important turning point in the suc-cession of seven-year periods. At twenty-one the spiritual birth takes place. We turn to this in the next chapter.

Moon node

Now we consider the important event which first com-
pletes its cycle during the nineteenth year, the moon
node. This event comes every eighteen-and-a-half years:
to be more accurate, eighteen years seven months and
about eleven days. There are forces that work into our
biography through the interrelation of the sun and moon.
Many of our natural rhythms are related to the cycle of
the moon. The orbit of the moon is at 5 variance from
the apparent movement of the sun as seen from the earth;
this results in a rhythmic course of changing relationships between sun and moon. It takes eighteen years
seven months and eleven or so days for all the positions
to be worked through: then comes the moment when the
'sun shines through' on to our biography; we are back in
our 'birth moment'. The series of positions begins to
repeat its cycle of variations until the next period of
eighteen-years-plus has been completed. This means that
the moon-sun position at the hour of our birth repeats
itself at approximately 18 years 7 months, 37 years
and 2 months, and 55 years and 10 months. These are
times when a new cycle takes over from the preceding
one, opening the opportunity for fresh impulses to be
taken up, with new directions in work and relationship
becoming possible: it is a time of crisis and renewal.
We may only realize later, when we look back on our
lives, how significant these moon-node times have been
for us.

So there is a moment at about eighteen-and-a-half
when the opportunity for new resolves is presented. This
is foreshadowed and followed over the weeks before and
after. At this first 'return' the decisive steps may be taken

in regard to the career to be followed or the set of values to be embraced.

In surveying a life-story one generally sees that this event has signified the end of adolescence. The person begins to take hold of the reins and drive his own chariot. It is time to clarify the first achievable goals and to start working towards them.

7. Entering the broad stream

Our exploration of the adolescent years leads us to the scenario of the early twenties. The twenty-first year heralds the ending of the seven-year period which began with fourteen. Twenty-one is the entry into adulthood; the person becomes responsible for what he does: the ego, the organizing entity, is now ready to take charge. The twenty-first birthday is celebrated with symbols of emancipation: from now on father and mother are older but equal companions and their relationship to their son or daughter needs to become one of adult-to-adult. The time when father tried to maintain his influence and mother her protection, which should have changed gradually during the teens, is now fully past. Indeed the father who tries to dominate his son or daughter into the twenties is courting a rift or else setting up an awkward dependency. If a mother tries to hold on to her son, she will seriously undermine his chances of a successful marriage; and it is somewhat the same for a daughter. If the twenty-one-year-old is still living at home, it is now high time for him to spread wings and take off to new vistas. He has to set out, prepared for what may meet him and what will be expected of him.

During the early twenties there is often education or training to complete, with exams to take for a degree or a qualification; then comes the transition into work and earning. Already by this time the person needs to have learnt to work: he must be able to apply his energies and thought-power to the task in front of him. In the twenties a person is judged largely by his ability to work. But work also gives him a sense of his own being; it expresses who he is, even if the work is not of his own choice. Kahlil Gibran says work is love made visible. Work implies physical or mental exertion: if we are open to finding satisfaction in what we have to do, and can become absorbed in it, this makes for contentment. Work may even help to dissolve a depression.

It is a paradox of modern life that we try to save time and energy in everything we do, with labour-saving devices enticing us on all sides, yet we gain far more satisfaction from whatever we achieve with our own effort. Unhappy is the young adult who does not wish to work or who cannot exert himself. The person who has not learnt to work either physically or with his mind by the time he enters the twenties will have difficulty in finding meaning in his life.

Working *solely* to gain money is not satisfying: it can brutalize even the self-employed person. There is an element of slavery in the system in which labour is treated only as a commodity. Fortunately this is being realized in work-management, which tries to consider the whole person. It can be wiser for someone entering employment to go for a lower-paid job which is fulfilling, rather than a job which is better paid but has nothing else to commend it. For those who want to free themselves from the wage-system, there are various working-communities like L'Arche, Camphill and some 'alternative' enterprises, in which the amount of money each member receives is not related to the work performed or the amount produced. In settings like these an attempt is made to separate work from the earning of one's livelihood: the individual works for the benefit of his community, and the community sees that he has the resources needed for his and his family's livelihood. This way he is not directly selling his skills and energy. Such a social interaction is possible only when the spiritual and ethical values of the community are reflected in the ideals of the individual who works in it. Many young people find this way of life more meaningful than the ordinary commercial world with its market-place for 'labour'.

So what work should the young person choose? One used to speak about being *called* to a profession or a craft: it was a vocation. So the question arises 'What calls one?' Each new generation is differently motivated from the one before: *security* used to be of paramount importance; now it is *meaning*. Meaning is not easy to find in a dully repetitive job, especially if there is no prospect of the worker moving on to more interesting and varied work: even when there is the prospect of better times ahead, the person may shy away from having to face a time when all he has to do is to repeat a simple operation over and over again. He may, however, have to accept an initial situation that falls short of his expectations, for training often requires doing monotonous work. In practice the young person may be obliged after all to do whatever will earn him a living — until prospects brighten.

Parents should not be worried if the entry of their son or daughter into working life goes rather experimentally at first: it is not unusual to try various occupations to begin with. There will be setbacks and tests, and also wrong starts: better to try out something that falls short of the ideal than to put off trying till the ideal presents itself, for this seldom happens. Entry into any career starts off uphill and asks for persistent effort: this is a challenge for any young person. But he is more likely to win through if he has foreseen what will be required of him and is prepared to apply himself to it.

Although the choice of career and the entry into work

have to be faced at the threshold of the twenties, the value
of travel that we ascribed to nineteen should be remem-
bered. If it has not been possible to travel at nineteen,
could this still happen in the early twenties? As we saw,
travel is not only geographical. It is also the journey of the
mind to gain enrichment, to make the universe one's own
and to extend one's horizon so that the world may be con-
tained in it. This is the world of ideas, of the great achievements of the human spirit and the tangible expression of the
divine in and beyond what is known. The person entering
adulthood should take the chance to spend time expanding
the content of his soul and deepening his reverence for all
that is, seen and unseen. In later years responsibilities for
job and family will restrict his wide-ranging search. He may
go on learning all his life, yet this would be enriched by his
having travelled and read widely and thereby having
learned all he could during these special years. Either way
the traveller can 'make the universe his own'. The early
twenties are full of potential if one is prepared to be *mobile:*
for these are the years of movement and of new experiencing.

One area of this dynamic is the forming of friendships
and the founding of relationships: of creating *philia* and of
kindling *eros;* of knowing what it means to receive the love
of a person whom one loves. Yet it can also be a time of
deeply-felt loneliness. The feeling that I am not important
or cherished by another person is usually unjustified: but
nevertheless this *feeling* of being uncared for is the reality
that has to be met. If I feel lonely, the chances are that it is
I who is not properly relating to *me.* Loneliness is a call to
deepen the inner life and so come to accept oneself. Worlds
of inner feeling, of thought and resolve can open if one
finds the way to transform loneliness into solitude. For this
to happen it is necessary to accept and welcome one's lone-

liness as a call to inwardness. Then the changes can happen.
Henri Nouwen writes:

> Instead of running away from our loneliness and
> trying to forget or deny it, we have to protect it and
> turn it into a fruitful solitude. To live a spiritual life
> we must first find the courage to enter into the
> desert of loneliness and to change it by gentle and
> persistent efforts into a garden of solitude. This
> requires not only courage but also a strong faith. As
> hard as it is to believe that the dry desolate desert
> can yield endless varieties of flowers, it is equally
> hard to imagine that our loneliness is hiding
> unknown beauty. The movement from loneliness to
> solitude, however, is the beginning of any spiritual
> life because it is the movement from the restless
> sense to the restful spirit, from the outward-
> reaching cravings to the inward-reaching search,
> from the fearful clinging to the fearless play.*

Once one has traversed the arid land of loneliness and
reached the meadow of solitude, there will be an experience
of inner spiritual calm. This in turn brings receptivity for
those who seek to share this calm in friendship.

The person who can accept truly and positively all one's
strengths and weaknesses, is the kind of person who could
become a life-partner. The question must be faced: 'Am I
ready to take responsibility for the life of another person
who will thereby be humanly dependent on me?' This
applies to a marriage or a co-habiting partnership. A relationship is never without its lasting effect. Whenever it

---

* Henri J.M. Nouwen, *Reaching out: Three Movements of Spiritual Life,* Doubleday,
N.Y. 1975; Collins, London 1976 (p. 35).

breaks it causes a wound. On the other hand if a relationship is continued without true communication, it slowly dies.

The forming of relationships in the early twenties therefore calls for much consciousness and right judgment: a path to walk with open eyes.

When a child is conceived but is not wanted, then the child is wounded, as well as the parents. The relationship of the parents should be established first, before introducing that which *needs* to be sustained by the relationship. This applies in the case of married couples, who do well to found their own relationship firmly before taking on the responsibility for a child. If a pregnancy happens where there is no marriage and no firm commitment to each other on the part of the parents, then decisions have to be made that have far-reaching consequences. When this happened to our teenage daughter, she was quite clear that there should be no abortion and that she would care for the child. The consequences of such a decision are never easy to bear, but they bring a compensation of their own. Termination of pregnancy also has consequences that are not easy, and the decision is an agonizing one. But one can say that the girl in this situation who decides to go forward with the pregnancy and accept motherhood may find herself sustained by new and deeper energies and will be able to experience inner satisfaction.

Thoughts like these call on those entering adulthood to nurture the aims, abilities and values which germinated during the teen years. Along with a leap forward in mental ability, there is the powerful emotional life, and a still-young ego to guide and harmonize the two into a unity of heart and head. It is the achievement of this unity that enables the person to be responsible and mature.

With this goes another vitally important step: the making of commitment. Marriage, career, religious belief, artistic endeavour, indeed anything that gives meaning and purpose to life requires commitment. The word has been much disliked; it suggests constriction: the thought of having no escape, except through copping out, is frightening. But commitment only looks harsh on the outside: it has a surprisingly beautiful crystalline interior. For commitment makes one free: free in the sense that it opens doors, reveals vistas, and gives scope for creative interaction with new people and possibilities. One grows in oneself and in one's engagement with life. Then the truth is experienced that what you gain from something depends on what you are prepared to put into it. The committed person who puts his whole self into his task finds that he experiences feedback. The one who resists commitment may pride himself on his independence, but he loses something of greater value.

As a person enters the twenties, one can wish for him to unfold in himself three regal gifts. The first is *honesty in his thinking,* so that he is able to distinguish good from bad, and to express himself with courage based on what he knows to be true. And so there develops JUDGMENT. Then *reverence in his feeling:* a revering of all that is, penetrating to the beauty inherent even in what appears ugly, seeing what is of worth in all things, and admiring the truth even if it is concealed behind ghastly distortions. This is the expansion of INTEREST. And the third gift would be *courage and determination in action,* which can help him to dissolve or move aside obstacles that still lie in his path. And so there grows MORALITY.

These three gifts would enable him to reach the goals he has set himself and fulfil the mission of his life; we explore them further in Chapter Nine.

8. New horizons

Adult man lives his life in a tension between opposing 'pulls' that try to take hold of his ego. The one is instinctive, the other is a pull towards a higher consciousness. The forces of the soul that are instinctive, acquisitive and demanding contain desires, volatile emotions and drives that impel him to satisfy his basic needs: they constitute a body of energy that urges the person to action or reaction. This is often called the astral body. Once it is somewhat tamed by culture and education, its colourfulness gives rise to the liveliness of the personality.

Then there is the higher ego or higher self. Its dwelling is in the spiritual world, and so it is not bound by earthly or physical limitations in the way that the 'ordinary' ego is. But it can shine into it, indeed draw near to it, inspiring and guiding it from its spiritual vantage point. In turn it absorbs from the ordinary ego a distillation of everyday life experience. The higher self is the eternal being of man, in touch with his angel: it is the identity that goes from incarnation to incarnation through the epochs of man's evolving. It is always inspiring and reassuring when a person is graced by an experience of the higher ego.

The astral attains freedom of action with puberty at about fourteen: this freedom is attained by the ego with 'adulthood' around twenty-one. So the ego is a step behind the astral during the teen years, and yet it has the difficult task of taming and subduing these forces at the height of their expansion and energy. This constitutes the basic reason for the stresses of this phase. Society expects the adolescent to keep the *astrality* within acceptable boundaries; the growth of freedom and authenticity of the person comes about when the ego itself determines, sets and reinforces those boundaries. In order to be able to achieve this, the ego has to be open to the guidance of the higher self.

Much that is culture is a taming and a sublimating of the astral forces in such a way that they find fulfilment through artistic endeavour and grace of movement and action. The more a person achieves cultural development, the less he needs to be kept within parameters of action enforced from outside himself. True cultural activity, which has artistic, aesthetic and religious components to it, opens the way for the higher self to become manifest in the life of the person. He becomes creative, free and self-activating; his deeds become infused with authority, and he wins the respect of his fellow men.

When we speak of a 'strong ego' in the true sense of the term, we do not mean by this a strongly assertive *personality,* as with a give-as-good-as-I-get 'macho' type or a self-opinionated egotist. For there is all the difference in the world between egotism and egohood. The egotist generally has a weak ego and tries to compensate for it by assertive or 'egocentric' behaviour. A person who is truly *ego-centred* is not *self-centred* in the sense of being selfish or conceited. A sign of an ego-centred person is that he is generous, unassuming, clear and inwardly strong: he has much to give and does so gladly.

For the grown-up person there are many spiritual exercises for self-development which strengthen the ego; sustained study also helps the ego to develop. So does the pursuit of some meaningful interest. There is further strengthening to be gained through the quality of interaction that comes about when he is aware of how he listens and speaks. He begins to participate creatively in conversation with others, listening sensitively, considering thoughtfully and responding with clarity. And there is, too, a benefit in terms of ego-strengthening if he learns to meet the crisis points that come upon him.

The higher self does not become part of our earthly existence: it remains in the spiritual state, relating to the incarnated ego but not controlling it. Deep in the feeling soul of everyone there lives a yearning to find the true companion, the *true spouse*. Naturally we tend to look for him or her in another human being, but even a very good marriage rarely assuages that longing to *meet* and *be met* in the fullest intimacy not only of body and life but also of soul and spirit. Much of music and art is the expression of this yearning, and a certain sadness pervades the soul when one realizes how far away the object of one's truest love remains. There is a tenderness in romantic music that soars into the heavens like Dante looking for his Beatrice. Poetry, music and song all point to the one truth. So do the Gospels: they tell of marriage feasts at which no bride is present, because they are initiations that unite the 'groom' or the 'son' with his own higher being.

Nevertheless there are times when our higher self draws nearer and shines more clearly into our souls, with a warm light that fills our heart and mind and our whole being. These are peak periods in our lives, the true high points. This is no false 'high' feeling, no escaping from reality: only a firm, gentle acceptance of what is, a sense of worth, and an energy to work in harmony with our highest aims. One can feel the higher self 'coming through' when one is filled with joy and gratitude. Or when one struggles through a tough assignment against heavy odds, and the solution is suddenly there, like a new creative force, exceeding one's wildest hopes. When this happens, one does not feel proud (that would be the astrality!) but humble, grateful and inwardly peaceful: these are wonderful moments.

Man's spiritual development is achieved to the extent that the ego is freed from the *bondage* of the astrality and finds a bonding with the higher ego. The higher self inspires our truest aims, but it does not constrain us to achieve them. Yet as this higher self is in touch with our guardian angel, this makes it possible for the light of the divine world to be conveyed to us on earth.

The healthy ego has a twofold task. It has to bring order into the astrality, making it subservient without diminishing its energy or colourfulness, and to strive to become open to the higher self and form a bond with it, so as to receive its guidance. This is the work of a life-time, but foundations are laid during the formative years of adolescence. The qualities that are brought into effect through this process will occupy us in the next chapter.

9. Three stars appear

Three qualities begin to weave into the life of the adolescent, as they also weave through the pages of this book. They are *judgment, interest* and *morality*. The higher self is beginning to shine through into the everyday life, and the pattern will become clearer as the teen years pass.

The motif that will characterize the person's life already begins to reveal itself.

Judgment

Growth of intellect opens the way to a good deal of critical analysis. The teenager may become hypercritical of his environment; he may altogether reject the order that he finds around him. His sensitivity leads him to defend himself whenever his actions are questioned, and to criticize others, at times unpleasantly or mockingly, even destructively. But he can be guided to observe more deeply and discern what lives within the soul of those he criticizes. Disdain can then give way to evaluating and understanding what is before him, so that he can take hold of its truth (as in the German *wahrnehmen*). This faculty will grow if friends, parents and teachers are prepared to listen to his opinions, however hurtful or scathing: for to be taken seriously will encourage him to think before he speaks, instead of merely giving vent to his emotions and criticisms. An assured hearing will make him more conscious of what he says. At times his criticisms may be far from emotional, coming rather from cold, dry intellect (less Luciferic, more Ahrimanic). But here too, given a respectful hearing, he will realize that cold reason has its limits and there are more things in heaven and earth than he has so far dreamt of.

This kind of inner dialectic will develop the power of judgment. It calls for unbiased observation and objective thinking: the person must put his own personality aside and open himself to the truth before him. It may be too early to expect this in an adolescent who has still to become firm in his feeling of selfhood, but the discipline of clear analysis and the effort to judge objectively will help him to establish himself as a more balanced person. As judgment develops, he will be able to weigh up relevant considerations, and he will then be able to welcome the opinions of others, recognizing that other people see the same thing from a slightly different angle. He will have realized that the interplay of varying opinions can allow the truth to emerge.

The teenager needs to become aware of when he is acting out of prejudice. Is he able to be open to ideas that do not accord with his own and to recognize the truth in them? Is he able to recognize his own prejudices? If a person rejects out of hand any ideas that do not support his own standpoint, his own ideas do not develop. Many factors combine to bring about the forming of right judgment, but the fundamental one is the awakening of reverence for the truth. When this faculty begins to develop in an adolescent one can indeed rejoice.

Interest

The second soul power to be developed by the ego can be termed 'interest'. The heart opens and receives. Before this can happen there must be a degree of selflessness, and the readiness to capture an idea, to get to grips with a project or to respond to the need of someone who asks for help: then the heart can reach out m confirmation and support. The person who is imprisoned within himself is not interested in the world around him and so cannot properly communicate with it.

The difference between judgment and interest is that judgment focuses on the phenomenon and evaluates it objectively, whereas interest is able to *enter into* the phenomenon and thus begin to grasp it intuitively. Asked to appraise a work of art, a person will be called upon to judge its merits as it is: however much the artist was under stress at the time, or had an ideal he was trying to express, the judgment must be on whether the piece of art itself is good or bad, successful or otherwise. *Interest* would then open the viewers understanding of the particular circumstances in which the artist painted it.

We may sometimes be justified in saying that we don't think much of the achievement of others, but interest helps us to appreciate *their effort.* Opening the mind and developing interest is a first step to bringing about compassion. Judgment confines itself to evaluating what is presented: but a judge who is learning to be human becomes aware of a further dimension. If he has the courage to take hold of this, he will discover new resources within himself which enable him to feel into the situation of another.

This new element awakens empathy and kindles the power of love.

The teenager needs to widen his interest in all the phenomena that he encounters. It is good if this does not blur
his judgment, for he has to seek the truth. But interest will
enable him to feel a kinship with what comes to him. He is
able in effect to say to a person 'I want to *know* you. I can
judge your actions as being good or bad, right or wrong: but
by knowing you I recognize what has made you do as you
did, and this helps me to accept you and your deeds.' Judgment calls up an objective assessment and engages our
thinking. Interest introduces a more subjective approach,
linking us both to the 'work of art' and to the 'artist',
allowing both to reveal themselves more deeply. Hence it is
important for parents, teachers and friends to awaken the
interest of the adolescent. And out of interest, love can
grow.

Morality

The third power can be called morality. The word is generally, even now, used in the sense of adherence to a set of
rules which have been handed down as the criteria of good
conduct. But goodness isn't achieved by submitting to reg-
ulation or to prescribed norms of conduct. Conforming
implies abiding by the *will of others,* whilst goodness
implies acting *freely.* Ideally each person should work out
his own standard of what is good, by truly listening to his
'inner voice'. Discussion with his peers and with others
whom he respects will help to sharpen his perceptions and
motivate him to look at the results of his actions and those
of others. It will also help him to recognize for himself what
makes sense and rings true, and what does not. If he
observes his reactions to everyday experiences and thinks
about them, he will gradually learn to listen to what they tell

him. Through this he will be able to create a 'map' of his own life-situation. With the aid of his 'map' he will be able to seek that inner response which could be called the 'voice of conscience'. Instead of listening to a stereotyped set of rules designed to condition his reactions, he will be able to go deeper and achieve an intuitive moral feeling. He is then more likely to act freely and truthfully, and to be guided purely by the ideal picture that arises.

Imagine that a young man has been invited to a party, at which the alcohol begins to flow. He has seen the effects on people when drink is taken in excess. He is keen to be part of the group and to join in. What is he to do? His own values will be called into question: he will have consciously to assess his situation and determine his course of action. In deciding what would be right for himself, he would also consider how he can assist the situation of the others present: there is always a social component to moral action. He might be able to ensure that everyone becomes more conscious of what they are doing, without moralizing but by remaining thoroughly social and involved. If he himself can act out of his own ideals, including his ideal of being social, his action will gain a certain authority: in respecting him, the others present will find themselves reviewing their own actions. Through this the others, individually, may well begin to act more consciously and freely, and so retain their own self-respect, in spite of the pressures of the party.

As this example shows, when a choice of action is presented, the young person will need to survey the various possibilities. He will need to discern what is leading him to his preference: is it a thought, an emotion or an instinct? In this way he begins to analyse what is motivating him. It could be that he finds that it is not clear: that there is a mixture of emotions and that he is confused or pulled in two directions. It may be that there is something that he *desires* but knows to be not right, so there will be at the same time the wish to do it and a holding back through a feeling of guilt. Often a person avoids admitting this kind of confusion, because it is uncomfortable and often means pulling back from what, in an instinctive way, he wants.

Once he has discerned what it is that is motivating him, he will have already begun to penetrate his emotions and instincts with thought, and by its very nature thinking brings calmness. This gives rise to the possibility that he will not be driven into doing something which he would afterwards regret.

This is a process of counselling oneself, for it is this that a counsellor does: he tries to find out the cause of the person's state of mind or the motive for his impulse or action. Then he seeks to bring clarity where confusion otherwise could be reigning. Clarity in its turn brings calmness, and if the person can face the choice calmly he is better able to be guided by his own ideals. Moreover he is less likely to feel pressured and can reach a view which he can feel is true. This guides him to carry out what he knows to be right. So he does not act out of the drive of his instincts or his emotions but out of his own process of thought and will. It is in this way that he will find access to a morality not based on stereotypes or rules.

This way of finding out what is right may sound ideal, but it is the way for modern man to develop his own freedom. Anyone can achieve this if he applies himself to it. When a person is able to guide and determine his actions in this way, his will is truly his own. This is a personal development which cannot be forced by others: but it can be encouraged by the example of parents and others, including peers, in the way they conduct their lives.

This process, at its best, would be fully conscious and deliberate. The shaping of one's values and the search for guidelines that can lead one to moral actions cannot happen without thought and effort. As these standards are applied in daily life, they become part of one's character. The moral impulse that we take hold of is the prelude to any true achievement.

A moral impulse arises in the soul when the higher ego is engaged and its light is able to shine into the conscious ego. Such a moment of inspiration can only be hoped for if the soul is ready and open. Abraham Lincoln, going through a slave-market as a boy, said to himself that if ever he became President he would stop this trade. Nelson's early sailing career was plagued by illness, and he almost gave up hope. But in what he called a 'sudden glow of patriotism' he resolved 'I will be a hero, and confiding in Providence, I will brave every danger.' The memory lived on with him until he died in the Battle of Trafalgar, with the words 'Thank God I have done my duty.'

Judgment requires the activity of *thinking,* backed up by the right feeling and strength of will.

Interest asks for the flowing through of our *feeling,* which can open the way for inspiration from the higher ego.

Morality seeks to bring light of thought into the *will,* so that we are able to assess our desires and our instinctive wants. In this way our doing is raised to a higher level of consciousness and is brought into harmony with our ideals. Even in tight situations we can then act deliberately and not out of impulse. All this makes it possible for our everyday life to be lit by our higher ego.

The teenager cannot achieve these three qualities without immense, continuous effort. While he was a child, the world revolved around him: he was in the centre of everything that happened. Now, as an adolescent, he needs to get beyond this, and widening interest helps to make this possible. As his morality grows, he becomes more aware of the world around him: he begins to be concerned about it. At the same time he becomes more conscious of the effect of his own actions, and he will not be tempted therefore to fulfil his own desires at the expense of others. With this he achieves what is needed to guide him towards his life-task. His aims will grow clearer with the passing years, and with the help of these three qualities he will be able to find the way that leads to their attainment.

Such is the ideal. It may be too early to expect this from the adolescent, because of his lack of life-experience. Yet when he attempts to enliven these three qualities, and is inspired and supported by those who have contact with him, his ego-strength will grow and he will gradually become ready for the tasks that await him in adulthood. He will be more equipped to consider the needs of others. And he will be better able to live his life in harmony with his own higher self and with the world around him.

10. Squalls

Sailing is not exciting if the sea is always calm and the wind set gently in the best direction. Contrary winds and squalls stretch the skill of the skipper and draw the crew closely into a team: the yachtsman learns how to cope and keep his boat floating and intact, and he achieves the mooring he was heading for. So also the teenager, together with his parents and all others who sail with him. The sail through the teen years has its exciting moments.

When the squalls come, it is vital to be practical. But we can also know that the weather will become calm again, and by then the squalls could have achieved a positive effect. With every crisis that is met and overcome, everyone concerned can become wiser and more compassionate.

So what kind of squalls can be prepared for, and how to keep a weather eye open? Try your hand at these.

Your child has struggled in school; she could not learn to read with the others. Now, after remedial teaching, she copes — just — but hates school. She is fourteen; school is compulsory till sixteen. She refuses to go on; you know she is distressed, depressed, and really unhappy. Her teachers have tried, but she refuses to relate to them: they support the idea that she should leave school because they find her disrespectful, obstinate and a disturbance to her class.

Your fifteen-year-old wants to change schools. You know there has been trouble in the group: there have been complaints about getting drunk at a school party. You discover that your child is about to be expelled. If you make the change immediately, you will pre-empt the disgrace of expulsion.

The young man who has been dating your seventeen-year-old daughter comes to your office: 'May I tell you that I took Jean to see my doctor, and he confirmed it; she is pregnant. I'm sorry to have to bring you this news.'

Your son is swotting for school-leaving exams; the pressure is on. You are steamed up because of all the money you have paid out for education at a private school; he had better pass! There is tension at home, tension at school; time is running out. And your son can't cope; he is near to breaking point.

The phone rings at home: 'Hello, Ma.' (It's your eighteen-year-old daughter.) 'Bad news; can't say much. Lucy and I are at Wynberg police station — they caught us, together with Jack, and we each had a joint on us. We're detained. We appear in court tomorrow morning. Can you come? May need money for a fine if we are not let off. Sorry, can't talk more. Don't worry; we'll be all right. Bye.'

How will you, as parents, cope with crises like these that suddenly beset your teenager and yourselves? These upsets can be extremely uncomfortable or challenging and could affect your reputation as well. Solutions could be arduous and costly. Once you are through the initial shock, you can draw comfort from the thought that an upset, however serious and shattering, nevertheless belongs to an unfolding life-pattern: but when the crisis assails you, it is difficult to be philosophical. It is no help if someone says to you 'Don't worry, for all will come right'. Nor is it the moment for well-meant words, with parent or teenager, about destiny and divine guidance.

There is a wound and it is bleeding; there are casualties who need help. It is just as well that the priest and the Levite went past the wounded man on the way to Jericho, and did not stop, for they might have regaled him with scripture texts to show that such calamities justly befall those who are sinners! Thank goodness the Samaritan was a practical person and immediately got on with treating the wounds.

Being prepared

There are various ways of reducing the risk of things going wrong: one way is to be open to discuss sensitive subjects, and show oneself to be unshockable and teachable. One needs to set high standards of integrity for oneself, and at the same time to have a warm heart that dispels any gathering greyness. Yet even so, like illnesses, the crisis times may be needed so as to alter a pattern or achieve a new resolve, a new plan, or better communication. Whatever occurs as a challenge to change oneself can be met creatively by transforming the negative elements into positive energies.

It is good to forestall crises, or at least reduce their impact, by heeding the early signs of a growing malaise, especially if the teenager himself gives a hint of increasing tension. The signs are not difficult to notice, the first one generally being a decline in communication: when a young person starts to draw into himself, it shows that something which he cannot handle is gnawing at him. The troubled look, the drop in spontaneity, a certain gloominess or surliness, all indicate that there is a problem. If he can speak about it, this will help him to think it through: but it may need gentleness and tact to present the opportunity in a way that he can accept. There is generally no need to give actual advice, and a good counsellor is not directive but encourages and helps the person to find the way to solve the problem for himself. He will be better prepared to meet the difficult time if he has achieved an image of himself that is not easily shaken; when things go wrong it is this that is threatened, because the teenager is so vulnerable. The caring or counselling person needs to weave into his whole approach an attitude to the teenager that fosters a feeling of personal worth. This will not be easy if the teenager has been through unusual difficulties in earlier childhood; but if it is not achieved in adolescence, the adult may be blighted for life.

When it happens

The moment a crisis occurs, parents as well as teenagers will ask 'To whom can we turn for help?' It is important to have a 'support group'. This means building up, in advance and consciously, a ring of people upon whom one can call. For instance such people as the parents' own brothers or sisters or other family members; or else neighbours or special friends, or the godparents. Then there are the more objective and more professional people who can be supportive, such as the minister or priest of their church, the general practitioner, the social worker, teachers, and the school psychologist. Or they may prefer to contact the telephone counselling service in their own area, if there is one, like Lifeline or the Samaritans.

With more serious problems, such as involvement with drugs, advice should be sought from agencies that specialize in this kind of problem. (This is dealt with further in the section 'Smoking marijuana', page 107.)

Parents should naturally first of all talk with each other: this is not as obvious as it sounds. Often mothers are left rather on their own, while fathers, for all their masculine leadership, are reluctant to take direct action themselves. A united approach is essential, mother and father in a harmonized endeavour to address the problem: at such a time it is especially important for the teenager to know that his parents are at one. They may first have to clear blocks and fill vacuums that have been allowed to come between *them,* a painful yet necessary process that can reveal differences in approach and feeling: so the problem of their teenager can have the effect of strengthening their own relationship, because it obliges them to share and to evaluate their attitudes with each other. It is as important for parents to get to grips with their emotional reactions to a problem as it is for the teenager himself to do so.

It is good if the teenager likewise becomes conscious of his own 'supporters'. Apart from his own parents — and the best friend if there is one — he may be able to turn to various members of the peer group, and siblings can often provide safe areas for sharing in confidence. Sometimes grandparents are just the people, and ideally the teacher would be a person who could help very relevantly. Another right person may well be a mentor or a priest or a social worker.

The suggestion that parents should develop a support group may sound a little artificial; surely, you may say, all this is obvious. Does one have to 'appoint' people to fulfil the role of friends in need? Well, for the sake of being prepared, yes. Those who would support you are not going to be reluctant to help: it is you who may be reluctant to ask anyone to help you. There is often embarrassment at having to ask for help, because it implies weakness or impotence and you may find it hard to reveal this. And so it is a valuable preparation, before any need arises, to get clear about the person or persons you would turn to in a difficult situation. The single parent is particularly in need of this; she or he may think 'it would be so much easier if I had a spouse with whom to share this': but strangely enough many 'well settled' couples could say that in fact, when it comes to facing family problems, there is all too little common ground between them.

Apart from this last point, which could well be contested (and how good if it were!), the parent, and in particular the single parent, is better placed to meet the squalls if he or she has in fact developed a number of friendships in which mutual trust and confidence, and also confidentiality, are assured. The assistance of the minister or priest of a person's church will be more readily enlisted if the parent has already come in contact with him and knows him well enough to be able to ask him to tune in to the present situation. Relationships of this kind cannot be taken for granted: they need work and openness.

Stress points

Now let us look at some of the situations that can cause stress to a teenager and require understanding and help. To begin with there are the happenings coming from outside himself which suddenly change his pattern of life: three main ones are a change of habitat when the family has to move to a quite different area; death in the family; break-up of the parents' marriage. Then there is a long list of occurrences that are personal — one could say private — to the teenager: which, however much they may involve others, are intimate issues. For instance the loss of a friend. This can be due to moving away, but it can also be the result of some newcomer entering the teenager's close circle and successfully rivalling him for the friendship of his own friend. It can also be one of those poignant experiences when one of the first girl-boy friendships ends with the friend going off with someone else. Break-ups of this kind — or even threats to the security and one-to-oneness of friendships — can be traumatic in the unsteady time of adolescence, when feelings are volatile and sensitive.

Then there are other problems that may arise. Activities and associations that previously were meaningful and engaging may lose their appeal as the teenage years pass. Belonging to Scouts or Guides may become stale, or a change in instructor may spoil the enjoyment at the riding or swimming club. Happenings like this can leave a vacuum in the life of a young person.

Troubles may arise in school. A slow learner may find it hard not to fall behind, needing extra lessons, remedial education, a change of school, or just interested involvement and encouragement from his parents. A plodder will generally get there in the end, but if he is really unable to keep up and fails repeatedly, some advice should be sought. Either way there is a situation to be addressed before the young person loses his self-esteem or is tempted to resort to subterfuges like bad behaviour or copying from others to cover up poor performance.

But it may happen that a pupil who is able to achieve well, and has been doing so, shows a sudden drop in the standard of his work for no apparent reason. It may not be easy to pinpoint the cause: it may lie deep down in the teenager's soul, and it may be something that can lead to disillusionment or even the breaking of his spirit. There was a very intelligent girl who at fourteen told her parents that she had made up her mind to study medicine and become a doctor. Her performance at school and her disposition were favourable, and it was an aim that inspired her. But her parents responded by ridiculing the whole idea: 'Do you expect us to meet the expense of your seven years of study, and then you just get married and it is all for nothing?' From that moment on her grades dropped and she had no ambition to gain good results, and her life since then has not been easy.

Whatever the circumstances, a drop in performance is always a warning to the parents to try and find out what has happened. It could be a sign that the teenager has entered the drug scene.

At the opposite end of the achievement scale there lies the problem that a pupil is too bright for his class and becomes bored. This can lead to negative results, and something should be done either to change the situation or to counsel the young person to enable him to accept it in a positive way.

A very different situation that throws up a problem is bullying at school. Peers can be very cruel, especially to someone who already suffers from a poor self-image or who feels he does not belong, for ethnic, religious, social or political reasons. An example of the last of these reasons can be drawn from the life of my brother. My family, though English, lived in Florence during my childhood, at the time when the Fascist regime under Mussolini was in full swing. My brother, who was already a teenager, went to the regular *Ginnasio;* there he was victimized by his teacher for being an *Inglese,* and the class joined in reviling him. After a while he was so broken by this that he had to leave the school and study by correspondence at home. Soon afterwards we returned to England, and a short time later he developed tuberculosis. An artistic person, he was more than usually sensitive, and this episode was traumatic.

The inner upheavals connected with the awakening of sexuality are a further cause of stress. (We have touched on this briefly in Chapter Five.) If a child is deprived of love in the family setting, it is more likely that he or she will have problems with sexuality. The teenager will obviously cope better if the home gives an example of good moral standards and if the parents show that they are open to speaking about the various aspects of sex. Sexuality becomes a problem when intellectuality and instinct form an alliance, excluding the heart. There is a mysterious relationship between intellect and sex: this used to be acknowledged in such expressions as 'a man knowing his wife' and is echoed today in the twofold meaning of the word 'conception'. When the mental activity of a young person is engaged in thoughts from the world of ideas, and in issues or questions that stimulate his moral feelings, his instincts will not be so likely to take over and fill his imagination. Boredom can have a negative effect; as can the bombardment of his senses by the media. A positive way to get sexuality on the right track is to develop the forces of the heart: a young person who can express his affection in caring for others will find the drive of sex less likely to overwhelm him, for then relationships become orientated towards giving instead of taking. True warm affection is considerate, tempered and patient: the child who has known real affection is able to grow into a teenager who is himself able to give affection in his own relating. If this was lacking in childhood, special help may be needed in adolescence.

The sexual force is a gift of nature and should be welcomed as such: yet just as nature has to be cultivated or else it wilts or runs wild, so also with the energy of sex. The three qualities of judgment, interest and morality, as we have described them in the previous chapter, can surround the emergence of sexuality with positive forces.

To be more specific: how would you as parents react to the news that your seventeen-year-old daughter has put herself on the pill? If this should have been a secret that you were not meant to know, how do you deal with the additional problem that you are not being granted open communication? This communication problem would need to be put right first, so that then the other one may be shared. Your daughter will, deep down, be glad if she can talk about her sexual questions with her mother, for she could be suffering from feelings of guilt and longing for a way to overcome them.

There are also other stress points, and two especially strong influences may sweep a teenager off balance. Strange to place them together, for they are drugs and religion. The drug scene is widespread, pernicious, expensive, destructive, clique-forming and addictive. Perhaps one had best not use all these adjectives for religious excesses: but there are dangers in religious zeal that can captivate people and draw them into a kind of irrationality that is akin to addiction. It is true that some quite emotionally engaging religious movements have rescued and rehabilitated young people who were heading for drug-addiction or alcoholism and wanted to become free of them, and there *needs* to be a strongly impelling conviction to effect changes in patterns such as these. Yet there is danger in religious practices that take hold of a young person and undermine his inner freedom.

If a teenager falls prey to either of these, what should his parents do? They should indeed begin by taking a positive interest in the religious attraction, and showing respect for it; with drug addiction they can at least be interested in how it has come about, and make it clear that it is just their respect for their teenager that makes them concerned. Whether it is drug addiction or religious excess, they should try to understand the appeal of this activity: they need to open their hearts. They will have to prepare themselves to see things through: but in the process they and their teenager will draw closer together, and he will draw closer to himself.

Smoking marijuana

It would take us too far to go into all the aspects of the drug scene. Some parents will have been through it themselves and so can speak from their own experience. Those who have not will need to learn about a world of strange happenings and perplexing contradictions. I would like here to confine myself to some aspects of smoking marijuana.

The smoker becomes more nonchalant but, deep down, more fearful; he (or she) displays arrogance and self-justification but knows that there is no *smoking* without *playing with fire:* he is heading for what could become an addiction. What begins as ego-boosting ends as ego-busting. And those who resort to heavier drugs may be courting disaster.

The drug-induced hallucination has nothing to do with true spiritual insight. The new generation experiences a longing for the widening of consciousness: and the drug culture distorts this longing by providing hallucinations.

We are contending today with forces that darkly obstruct the unfolding of the higher faculties in man. For instance *community* should have become a new hope for society, but communism has pre-empted it. The gradual emergence of a *caring society* has been undermined by the deadening effect of the bureaucracy of the welfare state. Such developments that should work for the progress of man are thwarted by caricatures which pretend to have all the advantages and claim to be the real thing, but in fact retard and block true development and draw innocent people into their power.

How can we understand the attractiveness of this grim perversion?

The modern adolescent is overwhelmed with facts at school and sense-impressions through the media: more than he can digest. They pour on to him like a torrent through school subjects, media entertainment and the intensity of city life. The longing arises to stop the world and get off. That is one feature. Alongside this there is today's emphasis on being an individual: this arouses his hope of a creative, independent style of life, and yet this is undermined by the prospect of finding himself in a dead end job. Caught in this situation, the young person says: 'No, this is hopeless', and searches for an escape: 'How am I to find relationship and understanding, communication and one-to-oneness with others when we are all destined to join the rat race? What's the point?' He looks out over the world of selfishness, ugliness, materialistic aims and violence, and cannot face it. He seeks instead for a means of finding harmony, joy, ecstasy, or at least a relief from pressure.

There is loneliness and boredom wherever the mechanical media have become a way of life. Neither tapes nor television nor any such passive form of entertainment can truly satisfy the absorber, because he has done nothing to create the sound or the content and only has to press a button. And what comes through is also not real music or voices but an electronic version of them. The joylessness, loneliness and hopelessness that beset the young person, in himself and in his environment, are reinforced by the ugliness and violence of much of the media content. How different from something created by oneself or being performed live for one to see and hear!

And so the wish arises to stop and dream, to find a world of harmony, or conjure up beautiful forms and colours that dispel cubic greyness; to expand, to grasp at some relief, an hour of respite. So it begins. And ends? Maybe it passes as a phase of experimenting. But, if it continues, the results can destroy will-power, concentration and self-respect. And the law can close in, harshly.

These paradoxes have to be faced by all who are confronted by the drug culture, and need to be faced by the teenagers themselves. You may not find out about your teenager's use of marijuana until quite some time after he has begun to smoke it. When questioned, there will come denial first, then a rejection of your right to interfere, a declaration that it is not a habit and he can give it up any time. If this is questioned he will assert that other acceptable 'addictions' such as alcohol are much worse. You may be able to bring him to the point where he promises to give it up: but you must know that this is not so easy, even if the promise is sincerely meant. To give up successfully asks for a change of leisure-style and companions.

The drug scene is pervasive and enticing. Parents should become informed about it and speak openly of its dangers, and about true ways of reaching spiritual experiences. This exploring can serve to 'unmask the opposing forces.'*

---

* See the small but very relevant book by L. F. C. Mees, *Drugs, a Danger to Human Evolution?* (Regency Press, London and New York, 1973)

Meeting this problem asks for a clear perception of the difference between the teenager as a person and the teenager's behaviour. The behaviour is up for judgment and possibly condemnation: not the person. For behind every surly 'smoker' there is a tender, anxious and struggling young soul. Although he presents a defensive front, he is calling out for a lifeline of understanding and love. 'Don't abandon me now' is what wants to come through. Maybe expert drug counselling is needed, but it is always important for parents to remain close to their teenager and support him warmly, in spite of what he is doing, because the drug scene can be terrifying for young people, especially if they are caught in the crossfire between the pushers and the narcotics squad. Within themselves too they are up against the crossfire between what they know to be wise and sensible, and the urge to experiment under the pressure of their peers. All this so as to escape from the world around them, which doesn't seem to be for them.

Seeking solutions

Finding a way through each problem is a creative process, generally asking for human interaction; people have to talk together. Their questioning, searching and clarifying releases an intuitive healing energy, and a note of hopefulness sounds; horizons widen and the understanding deepens. Then an idea may dawn; the new light brings warmth of courage, and the problem can be accepted and worked at. Those concerned have kindled their own inner resources to meet whatever has to be met.

Issues must be clear before ideas can form. This process requires 'quality time' and inner calm. Living in Africa teaches one to deal with bush fires. When you find a bush fire raging, it is useless to rush in and start beating it on your own: you have to let it burn while you call helpers together and decide on your strategy. You need to take into account the wind, the vegetation that is burning, and what is threatened by the advancing flames, and then to decide where to concentrate the effort. Maybe you will decide not to beat the fire at all but will rather clear a break some way ahead of the blaze, so that the fire will burn itself out when it gets there. Whatever the strategy, the main thing is to call in help before you are over-whelmed, and to think clearly, making a plan of action that appraises the situation calmly.

Many problems can be forestalled if teenagers can overcome their reluctance to share with their parents, and they will find this easier if the parents are able to keep pace with their development and the stages of the teenage scene through which they are going. The events in ado-lescence are dynamic: there are no frozen moments; there is no standing still. There is only movement: and it is always *forwards*.

So let us sum up with a few guidelines. When things go wrong there is a kind of ABC that may prove helpful. It begins with:

Accept the problem

Boil it down to its essentials

Clear your own emotions, acknowledging your feelings

Discuss it frankly with your son or daughter

Evaluate its seriousness

Form a picture in your mind of what each one concerned is going through

Generate warmth and understanding

Have a quiet time seeking inner guidance

Invite the help of persons whose wisdom and discretion you can trust

The more your teenager can share with you the better, for he will become clearer through expressing himself. It can happen that when he really opens up and acknowledges what is worrying him, he finds the solution himself through facing the situation squarely. But the problem he presents at first may only be an outer symptom of a much deeper one, which might require further delving: so it is important to know when to call in professional help. However, it is good not to make too great an issue of any problem: hence it is important to observe one's own reaction to see if it is really justified.

Sometimes finding a solution is not so easy, and it may take more talks for it to surface. Quick solutions often don't help in the long run: let assessment and evaluation be adequate, for then the solution will be more valuable. It is good to come to a definite plan, for something inevitably has to be done to dissolve the problem and its effects. When helping a younger teenager, the authority of the parents is still very relevant; the older teenager should feel called upon to find the solution himself. Either way it is important that the teenager should himself *believe* in the solution: otherwise it *won't* work.

As we have said earlier,* it may well be that the problem will have to be addressed by people other than the parents, if the teenager then feels more free to open his heart. It can happen that he will avoid speaking to his own parents when things are difficult, and will turn to the friend who has become his mentor. Parents may then feel excluded from what is going on. It is only too easy for feelings of resentment to arise towards a mentor who appears to be interfering. But if they can accept and understand, they will experience gratitude that at least

* See page 18.

their teenager has been able to open up to someone who can help. Such a feeling of gratitude may make it possible for the mentor to become a bridge between themselves and their wandering teenager.

Parents will find that they have to meet such problems with a great deal of love. It may be hard for them to avoid being judgmental: but it is good if they can avoid appearing 'holier than thou'. Adolescence is a growing process, and the many adjustments needed on the way inevitably throw up problems: but the occurrence of problems is evidence of change, and their right handling can translate them into valuable life-experience.

All may be well in the teenager's surroundings and in what he is achieving, but his world is constantly changing. With the emergence of his new identity, he feels different in himself and so relates differently with his parents: he becomes less involved with them and therefore more on his own. He can feel exposed, unsure and incomplete through the loss of framework and the increase of freedom. He may find that he is alone as never before. Physical development may bring with it a measure of self-assurance, but this is on the outside. Within, he experiences a gnawing sense of inadequacy, due to his uncertainty about himself, and there is tension between what is growing in his inner world and what is happening in the outer one.

Because he feels alone it is not easy for him to share his inner experiences with another person: it is not easy to hand over to another, even to a parent, the chance to gaze into his emptiness and confusion. In opening himself he feels how vulnerable he is: he exposes his weakness, which is hard for his self-esteem and may make him feel humiliated. In rare moments he will be really open, and parents may see this as an opportunity to teach him something. But they need instead to hold back, and rather surround his anguish with love.

An older teenager, in the way he expresses himself, may tend to be abrupt, impatient, unreasonable or disparaging. But for the moment this is his only way of expressing his impulse for independence, and it is vital to avoid undermining this impulse. This doesn't mean that one has to tolerate bad behaviour. But one gets further if one can hear, through it, that he is saying: 'Please don't submerge me; I am trying to become a free person and I am having to struggle. And just now I'm feeling smothered and I can't help reacting'.

This longing for independence is a main reason for the way an older adolescent often rejects directive advice: for this puts him into a dilemma. He can't allow himself to consider whether the advice is helpful: he only sees it as an unwanted intrusion on his freedom. He dislikes the idea of succumbing to authority: if he follows the advice, he is doing what others have prescribed, and therefore is not acting freely. If he rejects the advice in order to assert his independence, he kids himself that he will feel free, though he finds he doesn't. How often a person will look back on his own teen years and tell his parents: 'I know what you told me was right, but I couldn't accept it then'.

This means there is another factor we have to bear in mind in going along with our teenage sons and daughters. The adolescent can hardly avoid going through times of confusion, although he may not be aware of this. It is difficult for parents to understand why a teenager reacts the way he does. Their only guideline is to try to meet him where he is and not where they think he should be. This means respecting his bewilderment, because it belongs to his struggle to sort himself out.

Keeping involved

When things go wrong, therefore, parents have to become involved and may also need to involve others as well. To take the line of: 'He's brought it on himself — now he must get on with it' could court disaster. It would also be neglecting an opportunity for showing interest and love. Crisis times and problematic situations can have the effect of bringing people together, parents and teenagers and those around them: all in some way gain from the opportunity to show that they care for each other.

Communication and understanding are necessary. So is confrontation. The good listener enables the young person to tell of his feelings and perplexities, and thereby see them more clearly. The listener himself does not confront, but by holding up the mirror he enables the young person to confront himself and become his own judge of his intentions and actions: and this is more truly a confrontation than giving him a burst of one's feelings. The teenager can grow by confronting himself; he can't grow by confronting his parents' emotions.

What is here advocated is not softness but firmness, not conceding but understanding; not merely tolerating, but trying to transform each situation into the positive. If one becomes angry with a teenager because of unresolved tensions within oneself, the teenager will justifiably resent what comes towards him. But deep in his soul he can respect the righteous wrath he meets when he has let himself down and has caused others to suffer because of his thoughtlessness and selfishness. When the young man told me that my sixteen-year-old daughter was pregnant, I managed to retain self-control — just: yet I found myself speaking with a strength and an earnestness which

I have seldom plumbed. Such resources one finds within
oneself when issues of life are touched.

So it is with adolescence — one touches issues of life.

11. Coming alongside

Two worlds open for the adolescent: the outer and the inner. The outer world brings him into contact with all that goes on around him; it is full of encounters with people, with many who would teach him. It is a demanding world of activity, and at times he will feel connected with it and fully absorbed by it; at other times he will feel estranged from it. He will have many relationships: not only the given ones with his family and his teachers and school companions, but also with those whom he will seek out for their special qualities. Yet some of these will disappoint him and others cause him distress. There will be times when he feels himself cut off and alone: he will look at the scene around him and be unable to join it, until some opening or an outstretched hand involves him again and the loneliness disappears. There will be times when he will even want to be alone, in order to draw new strength from study or from the developing of his personal skills, so that he will have more to give in the future.

But there is another loneliness, which has to do with his other world: with the *inner space* that rises within him during these teen years. This is the world of inner feeling and of being conscious of his own Self. From this space come his deeper inspirations and inner guidance that will help him to make decisions and meet those problems that touch the values that he wants to uphold. It is because it is so personal that it is not easy to share with others what lives in this inner world. During these years it is developing and still tender, and it constitutes a new territory in the experience of the young person. This inner space can seem insignificant in comparison with the strength and certainty of the outer space: and it can seem so far removed from it that the young person may feel that he can't live in both and must choose in which to live. It is a space that is not based on facts or forms that are given: it is as though everything has to be allowed to grow, and it needs sensitive contemplation in order to recognize *what* is growing there. It is a holy place, and what it contains can never be fully known even by the young person himself. The ideas that arise in it can be very great, filling him with hopes about his province in life, even though the prospects may seem daunting. It is dynamic and ever-changing and leads the young person through high peaks of joy and deep troughs of sorrow: it is the place where he becomes aware of his own selfhood but also knows that this is vulnerable. What lives within this space is not for public view: any invasion will be experienced as violation, and will bring with it the fear of ridicule. If ridicule occurs the person may be deeply wounded and can react by denying this space, closing it off and concentrating on outer activity which does not require him to be so conscious of himself: but in doing this he actually denies himself and avoids meeting himself, and so ceases to care for what is truly his own.

The young person needs to be encouraged to accept this space within and to dare to explore it. To be able to share this exploring with someone else helps him to find out what is there: but this other person must realize that he is being let into a very personal place, still in the process of becoming, and that it is a place he has to honour as being intensely meaningful to its owner. Such a person would have first of all to know and accept his *own* inwardness, as well as being healthily involved with the world of outer activity.

One who is allowed into this inner space is in effect coming alongside: he is both meeting and being met. The adolescent longs to be met and to be affirmed there where he is busy with his own creation. But it is rare for a young person to be met in this way, for there are all too few people who develop in themselves the revering attitude, the sensitiveness and the selflessness which ideally are needed if one is to enter the sanctum of another person. These qualities are indeed the marks of humanity and form the basis on which true relationships are built: they have to be worked for, but no one should feel that he cannot achieve them. Even one who is still aspiring to this sensitivity may find himself called upon to enter the inner space of an adolescent, and although not ideally prepared, may already be able to gain admission and relate to him there. He needs however to be able to acknowledge his own potential for growth, and to have a yearning for wholesomeness in his own being. This will help him to enter without misunderstanding or violating. He then has to put aside his own aspirations, ideas and worries and be warmly open to what the young person shares with him.

Some ignition point is needed to spark off a new relating, and it often begins with one person wanting something from the other. This can indeed work both ways, for it can be very affirming to a seemingly less endowed person to be asked for help by one who is more endowed. When Jesus was in Samaria he sat down by the Well of Jacob and there he met the woman: their meeting began with his asking her for a drink (John 4:7). Meeting can only be on the basis of full mutual respect. A person who has achieved progress in his inner life should not wish to meet the adolescent in order to *help* him; this would be condescension. We sometimes use the term 'levelling', and this is a good term because it means that this kind of meeting affirms the equal worth of both. The teenager longs to have his world affirmed, but he is usually surrounded by those who would *teach* him and *guide* him and *pick him out* on his failures and *assert his need to learn.* This may be appropriate in the outer world, though even there the teenager will learn more from the adult who is able to correct him without making him feel inferior: meeting in the inner space, however, does not have the motive of bringing about change but of *affirming.* In fact it will bring about change, but in a different way: there will be no teaching, but the adolescent will grow through what he experiences in such a meeting.

The person who can *meet* the adolescent respects that eternal part that is gradually unfolding in him. The ability to listen and to speak out of one's own deepest feeling enables a true meeting to come about, and the sign of its being achieved is that *both* discover new depths in themselves. Impulses and aspirations which until then had lain dormant within them are awakened. Areas of thought and feeling which had been overlaid by insecurity or confusion now become visible. The good listener can awaken sleeping memories and throw light on tangled experiences which one had tried to forget. How wonderful it is when one can at last dare to tell a person what one has never dared to say to anyone before!

Such is meeting and being met.

It gives reassurance. It releases energies to strive for the ideals one cherishes. It affirms the qualities that the adolescent is secretly nurturing, hidden from the view of those who would not understand. To be met in this way can be of lasting significance for the adolescent, because it enables him to accept his own innermost self and to go on exploring it and finding its worth. Ideally such meetings should not be isolated but recurring, if the adolescent is to grow into a full-strength adult.

Within this space there can be manifest something that transcends the individual. It is the 'I', but it is more than 'I': for it is here we touch humanity itself.

When the young person is discovering his own humanness, his own depth and potential, and this is affirmed by an understanding friend who meets him in this way, he will be able to meet the world outside him, with courage, acceptance and reverence. But if no one meets, affirms and encourages him, if no one can be allowed in because he does not trust himself to be open or trust any other person to come so close, this part of him is in danger of withering. His life could then become little more than one of reacting to what comes to him from outside, or else he will shut himself up with his own inner life, and his contact with the world will become an unreal play-acting, giving what is needed but not giving himself.

The young person who has been *met* will not forget this meeting, and its value will live on with him: it will sustain him in his life. But it needs those who have at least begun to develop the qualities that enable a true meeting to happen. It is no criticism of a parent if he or she is not yet able to respond as such a friend: this is bound to be easier for someone who stands a little apart and can see the adolescent freshly and not as the child-who-was. On the other hand it is natural for a parent to want to be accepted in this way, and good if this can happen.

People with these qualities are particularly needed in our age, which sets so much store by individualism and self-dependence. Everyone knows that 'communicating' is the answer, but only such people know the secret of true communicating.

Those who are truly met in their teen years will have more feeling for meeting others as their life proceeds.

12. Mooring

Open the family photo album and see how it tells the story of our theme. Follow the changes year by year: recall the moment when your oldest entered the teens, and how the others followed. Observe how the pictures show a change each time, in each of them, till one by one they reach the twenties. A powerful story will unfold before you, as strong and as beautiful as the coming of spring.

However far your children are in this whirl of growing, they are taking on new forms and substance all the time. You will feel how quickly the next stage presses in. The photos recall difficult phases, celebrations of achievement, and times of relaxation and reunion. You witness change in your teenagers: the photos show the burst of freedom and the narrowing down towards commitment, as year by year the new person emerges in each one.

As you accompany and support them you feel the change in yourselves as parents. Yet as parents you provide the still centre around which they make their various expeditions into new territory.

You make the difference for your children, and your companionship is vitally relevant. Never succumb to the feeling of being bypassed, discarded or not needed! They will tell you later how much your faithfulness meant to them: and your discipline. You will have proved all this

by the way you had to work on yourselves to keep going.
Especially you will have proved your love.

The teen years are the time when one first falls in love.
For parents this time is the school of loving.

Friends and Lovers

Working through Relationships

Julian Sleigh

A sensitive look at the issues surrounding friendship, intimacy and loyalty in the modern world.

Taking as his theme the fulfilment of the Self through encounter with the Other, Julian Sleigh discusses the joys and pitfalls of people searching together for meaning and happiness in relationship. Friendship, love, marriage and divorce, 'from rapture to rupture,' are all explored, against the background of modern western culture in which, for many men and women, social and sexual roles are being perplexingly redefined.

Floris Books

Crisis Points

Working through Personal Problems

Julian Sleigh

As a counsellor, Julian Sleigh has helped many people through a crisis in their lives. He has distilled these years of experience into a process of twelve steps which help to resolve difficult situations of all kinds. These steps are designed to allow us to face the facts of our lives and to perceive the feelings and emotions that come from our own destiny.

Floris Books